SURVIVING TRAUMA

SURVIVING TRAUMA

TACHIANNA ORTIS

Surviving Trauma

ISBN: 978-1-7334723-6-4

Printed and bound in the United States of America.

Editor: Erick Markley
Development Editor: Roszien Kay Lewis

Confessions Publishing is a subsidiary of Roszien Kay LLC, Lancaster, CA 93536

For information regarding discounts on bulk purchase and all other inquiries, please contact the author directly at tachianna27@gmail.com

I, Tachianna, am her. . . the one who
Survived Trauma. . . These are my truths . . .

CONTENTS

PREFACE

I struggled with writing this book. I didn't want to tell people the good, the bad, and the ugly things that happened in my life. But every time I got on my knees to pray, the Lord kept telling me to write the book. I tried to ignore Him. I argued with Him over and over again.

I was fearful. I didn't want to be judged by others. I was afraid of being laughed at. I was fearful of how people would look at me. I was fearful of the unknown. I was also afraid of writing. Writing made me feel extremely uncomfortable. I never graduated from high school. Honestly, I had very little schooling, by no fault of my own. I couldn't understand why God would want me to write a book telling my innermost personal life issues. Especially when I had blocked out so much.

Although I was uncomfortable, I pushed aside how I felt and decided to obey God and write my story. I would go weeks without even trying to write. But God wouldn't let up. Every day, writing this book would be in the back of my mind. I would literally hear, "did you write today?" I heard it so much that I thought the Lord was crazy!

I started to question God, and remind Him of the fact that I had only one hand. Before I could move on with any more excuses, my sister in Christ, Laquitta, gave me a tablet. Now I couldn't use my hand as an excuse because all I had to do was speak into the tablet and it would write for me.

Next, I tried to give God the excuse that I didn't have an editor. My sister Laquitta pointed me into the direction of where I needed to go. Even after this, I had different people offering to pay for an editor. But the Lord told me to go with the one my sister pointed me to.

God literally made it too easy for me to continue to drag my feet. He literally handed me everything that I needed. The only thing that was left was for me to fully obey Him. So I decided to finally take my life back. I stopped making excuses. I stopped listening to the devil, and reminded myself that no matter what he said to me, I had to obey God and write. I wrote the vision and made it plain as day. I sat back and watched God work through me.

As I wrote, I literally had to take time to remember things. I had to relive and face the pain. I had to come to a realization that as painful as it was at times, writing this book was necessary. Yes, I had to put all of my faith in God. But it was still necessary. The process made me deal with so many emotions. I was forced to deal with what I didn't want you to think. I was forced to deal with the fact that after reading my story, some wouldn't see me as someone who was always in the church. Some would see my truth.

I have been delivered from a lot of things. In the proceeding pages, a lot of things are going to come to light that nobody knew about. As you read my story, you're going to see many different sides of me. Sides that I'm honestly not proud of. You're going to read about things that I have done that I'm not proud of. But you will see my truth.

With writing this book, I've decided it's time to start being honest. Therefore, I'm going to say how I felt. I'm going to expose the things I've had to endure. I'm going to expose the things that I have done. I will no longer lie. I know my story is not for everybody. But it needs to be told. And I've made the choice to no longer try to sugarcoat the traumatic things that I've been through.

For many years, like many others, I sugarcoated my truth. I walked through life in silence acting like nothing ever happened. I did this because I was too ashamed to admit the whole truth. I did this even though deep down I had been shattered to my core. The truth is I didn't know how to overcome the continuous thoughts that haunted me . . . thoughts which were played over and over in my mind.

I must warn you now, my story will be very graphic. At times even x-rated. But these are my truths, I experienced childhood molestation. As a result, the majority of my life I was bound by sex. I continually thought that it was going to get me ahead in life. I threw my body around like some leftover piece of meat. I'm overcoming sex addiction, molestation, alcoholism, rape, having a pimp, being a stripper, physical and mental abuse, adoption, a disease that took my right arm, losing my children and more . . . These are my truths!

As I write this book with tears, regret, and anger, I write for all my broken sisters who have secrets. I have survived all my adversities so that I can write to the places you are most hurt. As I write, I write the things you are ashamed of admitting. I write to put to shame the people who called you a liar; to the people who didn't believe you. I write to expose those things that you're living with secretly; to break the bitterness that's been holding you down. I write to the extra baggage you may still be holding on to.

I write my story to tell yours. . . The times when you were raped, beaten, or mistreated as a child. Even those times when it was done by a loved one. I write to help you heal from the times when nobody was there for you. For every moment when you just couldn't figure out why nobody loves you. I write to let you know that you are not alone.

I believe once you start reading and seeing how much I've overcome through Christ Jesus, you'll realize there is hope for you. As you turn each page, you'll start to see that you too will be able to overcome all of your trials and tribulations. You'll realize that when you come to Jesus, everything isn't going to be perfect. But you'll quickly realize that everything is going to make more sense as you work through and get through those hard times. All while knowing that you have a God who is fighting for you.

No matter what trauma has happened to you, or what you've survived, you must understand there is a deep calling on your life. No weapon formed against you shall prosper. There's a reason why your life has been hard and unexplainably painful. Beautiful things develop from dark places

Lord, as you have given me strength and guidance to write this book about my trauma, I ask that you use it to help heal other women. That you use it to help them understand that they aren't alone. I ask that through this book, healing takes place in her life. That she begins to believe that she is beautifully and wonderfully made despite her trauma. And lastly, that she begins to understand that You have not forsaken her. In Jesus' Name, Amen!

God loves you. . .

CHAPTER 1: FOSTER CARE

My birth mother was a tall beautiful woman with colored eyes. She was a drug addict, prostitute, and stripper with a third or fourth grade education. I was told from a young age that she was a whore, and that she had a lot of issues, without ever being told by anyone what those issues were. Even though I was young, I did not like how everybody around me would talk so negatively about her.

My older brother and I ended up in foster care because my mother left us. Before I was born, my brother, who is a little more than two and a half years older than me, had been taken by our 16-year-old mother to a babysitter. Instead of my mother picking him up within a reasonable time, she left him for days as she got her "fix" and made her money. After caring for my brother for days, without knowing if my mother would ever return, the babysitter had no other choice but to call CPS. Once CPS was involved, my brother was placed in foster care.

Three years after losing her first child to foster care, my mother gave birth to me. I'm not sure how the first two years living with my mother were. I don't have any memories to share. The only thing I know is that my mother took me to, and left me with, the same babysitter whom she left my brother with three years earlier. Because she left me with her for far too many days like she had done with my brother, the babysitter called CPS.

Once I was placed in foster care, my father could have gone to court to get me. But he didn't. He thought that I was living with my

Puerto Rican grandparents. Which he was fine with because he was too busy running around the east side of Las Vegas selling drugs. Little did he know that I was in foster care from the age of 2-4 years old.

Being placed in foster care at a young age was interesting. I don't remember a lot except for a few things. Like standing in a crib crying my eyes out. Apparently, someone used to talk to me a lot because the first language I had spoken was French, not English. Because of this, I had to later learn English.

By the age of 4, I had been to around 10-12 foster homes. There were times when I lived in the same foster home as my brother. Then there were times when my brother and I lived in separate foster homes. Eventually, they decided to keep us together. The times we were separated we were pretty bad.

The bond that my brother and I had I was told started at a young age. We had such a tight bond that we developed our own language. A language that nobody else knew or understood but the two of us. Apparently, we would sit and have full-on conversations.

Even though I was very young while in foster care, I still remember certain homes or certain situations that happened. In one particular home, I remember we were not supposed to be outside alone with the dog. On that particular day, I remember a black woman handing me the popsicles, and an older tile floor. My brother was outside alone with the dog. After getting the popsicles, I showed my brother his. My brother came running to the door. For whatever reason, I slid the glass door shut. I thought it was funny that I had a popsicle and he didn't.

As he stood outside with the dog, my brother bent down and touched the dog's foot. All of a sudden, the dog clamped onto his head. I remember screaming, "here's your popsicle, here's your popsicle," not understanding the seriousness of what was going on. I watched the dog drag my brother around the small slab of cement we called a backyard. I stood there just screaming and screaming, seeing the black dog and its teeth on my brother's head. I knew it was all my fault!

The dog eventually let go of him. My brother was left with a huge scar on his head. As a result of what happened that day, we were both traumatized at such a young age. We both thought all big dogs would bite us. At that time, if we would see a dog, we would take off running because we were so scared. To this day we both are not dog people.

As my biological mother sat in prison, she called her estranged parents (her biological father and step-mother) who knew nothing about us. She wanted them to come and rescue us from foster care. At that time, I had to be at least four years old, and my brother had to have been almost seven years old. Even though they didn't know us, they came and got us.

Unbeknownst to my mother, they had no intentions of keeping us permanently. In fact, they were trying to find us a home with another family. My grandparents didn't want to be parents. They just wanted to be Grandma and Grandpa. Shortly after being with my grandparents, we were placed with a black family. We didn't stay there long because my grandparents took us back. They said that they knew the family was just in it for the money.

After returning to live with our grandparents, we started to bond with them and other family members. I, unlike my brother, had a close bond with my grandpa. He was a true foul mouthed thick accented Puerto Rican. He was tall, very dark, and funny. He was often mistaken for a black man until he started to speak. I remember how he loved to wear linen and hats. And how much he loved me. He spoiled me. My grandpa was my everything.

Unfortunately, this wasn't the case for my brother. My grandpa was extremely hard on him. I remember my grandpa would hit him a lot with the belt. He was always yanking off his belt as quickly as he could. He did this while screaming in his thick Puerto Rican accent as he lifted out of an old brownish rocking chair running. My grandpa would literally run down the hallway after my brother just to hit him.

Favoritism took place a lot with my grandparents. My brother and I were never treated the same. On one particular day, we went to the grocery store with our grandparents. I was allowed to ride the little toy car outside of the store, but my brother wasn't.

While this was going on, my grandparents continued searching for a suitable, stable, long-term home for us. The failure of the first foster home did not stop them either. By this time, they had grown certain that they wanted something more like an open adoption. My grandparents wanted to be able to make phone calls and have the ability to visit us sometimes. They wanted to be able to send gifts and things of that nature. They didn't want to get rid of us completely, they really just wanted to be Grandma and Grandpa.

After some time of searching, they found an adoptive home. Once this happened, we started talking to people on the phone. They even started sending pictures back and forth. What I didn't understand was that we were being groomed to live with this family.

My grandparents had prepared us by explaining to us that we were going to have new parents and a new brother. At the age of 5 and 8 years old, I don't feel like we truly comprehend what was happening. After being told, my grandma, brother, and I were on a plane to meet them.

The day we left was strange. I remember how quiet my grandpa was. He really didn't say much to us. Thinking back to that moment, I don't believe it was his full intention to give us up. Rather, I believe it was something that my step-grandmother wanted because she hated my mother. Nevertheless, my grandpa allowed it to happen.

We met a tall dark-haired social worker at the airport that day. After meeting her, we drove for what seemed like a very long time. During the ride, I recall the social worker continuously talking about how wonderful our adoptive family was. As she spoke, I sat in the back seat looking out the window feeling a little scared.

After about an hour drive, we arrived at our destination—a little old town of nothing. The town literally was just dirt, sagebrush, and a bunch of mobile homes. There wasn't even a Walmart, any type of fast food, or anything in sight.

We pulled up to a big nice mobile home. It had two living rooms, 3 bedrooms, and a very big backyard. After getting my big old brown suitcase from the back of the car, I remember walking up a number of stairs to meet my new mom, a short white lady with dark brown hair. And my new brother, who was very hyper and excited to finally see us. I wouldn't meet my new dad until later because he had been working.

After seeing our new rooms, I went back to my grandma while my brother ran around with our new brother. I stood next to my grandma for quite a while as everyone talked. I listened as Grandma told my new mom about the foods we liked and didn't like. The only thing that we really liked were SpaghettiOs. I listened as my grandma explained to my new mom how to do my hair. I listened as she told her that I liked my nails done, but not to paint them red because red was too grown-up.

As they talked, I remember being scared. Honestly, I was a little confused. Yes, the lady seemed kind of nice. But I didn't know her. I knew my grandma. She took care of me. Even though I was never very fond of my grandma, I knew her. She obviously took care of me. I didn't want to be out of her sight.

But I had no control. After they talked, she hugged me, said goodbye, and left us. I stood at the window and watched the only person I had known in this strange place drive away without me or my brother.

At that moment, I felt panic. I wondered how someone could just leave us here. From an early age, I remember feeling the spirit of rejection. I always felt like people were going to leave me. It's as if rejection had been trying to break me down since I was a young child. At a time when all of the cards were already stacked against me.

Even though I was so used to everybody leaving at that age, I couldn't understand how you could love somebody and just leave! I wouldn't learn the answers to these questions until 14 years later.

As a child, I had no idea what destiny assassins were. I did not know that the devil would send certain spirits to try to hold you bound so that you wouldn't reach your destiny. The devil didn't play fair then, and he still doesn't now. He has always been out to get me. He has always desired to hold me back from my true calling in life.

Matthew 19:30- "but many that are first shall be last; and the last shall be first."

CHAPTER 2: MY NEW FAMILY

As I stood in a panic as I watched my grandma drive away, my brother was unbothered. It's as if he didn't notice that she was gone. He happily ran around with this other kid, our new brother. I remember being a little jealous by this. He was my brother. I didn't want to share him. He was the only thing that I had left.

Even though I wasn't happy to share my brother with my new brother, I understood why they meshed well. My new brother was funny. He was outgoing. He was hyper too. All of these attributes made it easy for them to bond quickly.

Speaking of bonding, I was able to bond with my new mother too on the first night. After she started dinner, I helped her set the table. As we moved around the table, I remember how she made an effort to get to know me better. With every response, I remember wondering if she liked me. The five short years of being rejected so many times had already taken its toll on me.

Despite what I felt inside that night, I continued helping as I moved around the dining room table and in the kitchen. In that moment, I no longer felt panic. I actually enjoyed being a little helper.

The enjoyment I felt spilled into every moment of that night. As soon as my new dad came home, he immediately began bonding with us. Before this moment, we didn't have a dad to bond with us the way our new dad did.

That night, he playfully threw us around the living room. He'd put us on his legs and fling us over his head. Although my brother was used to this type of horseplay, he too became stiff and kinda scared. But neither one of us complained. We continued to fill the house with a lot of laughter and endless smiles.

Unfortunately, the laughter and joy we experienced that night wouldn't last forever. I learned very quickly that my new family was strict. They had a lot of rules. Everything had been scheduled to the point we were like little soldiers. We were given commands like brush your teeth, wash your face, comb your hair, and go to bed on time.

Their way of parenting was very different for us. Up until that point, things had been different in the foster homes we had been in. Things had even been different with my grandparents too. Honestly, before this point, I don't ever remember having dinner together as a family. Or having to eat certain types of food.

Before, if I didn't like a certain food, it wasn't a big deal. No one had a problem with me eating whatever I liked no matter how often I ate it. I was allowed to eat SpaghettiOs and ravioli without punishment. I'm not saying that they were the healthiest food to eat. But not being able to eat them like I had at my grandparent's house was strange.

I quickly learned that living with my new family was a whole new ballgame. They ate very healthy. In fact, a lot of what we ate was from our garden. In their home, we couldn't leave the dinner table until our dinner was done, or until you at least tried a bite of food. Oftentimes, I sat staring at what was placed before me thinking, "I don't want this." Being the picky eater that I was, I would literally gag on almost any and everything served for dinner.

Food wasn't the only difference I had to now get used to. We had to get used to having a dog around. One day as we played outside, the neighbor's dog ran into our huge backyard. As soon as my brother and I saw a big dark brown dog running up to us, fear instantly took over. My eyes bulged from my head; my hands went flying in the air as we screamed while trying to run to the house.

Although time had passed between the last attack and now, fear of being attacked again was still there. We were still traumatized by dogs. Instead of being understanding and comforting, our new mom showed us no empathy. Instead, she thought we were being ridiculous. She wouldn't allow us in the house. She actually grabbed us and made us touch this dog. She did this as she repeatedly told us that we didn't have a reason to be scared.

I guess she really didn't comprehend what we had gone through. I literally saw my brother's head in a dog's mouth with blood all over the cement. And I felt like it was my fault, and I didn't want it to happen again. Eventually, we did get somewhat used to having dogs around, even though I was always looking over my shoulder.

Because she trivialized our fear of dogs as being ridiculous, I felt like nobody cared about what we had already been through. We had been through a lot at such a young age. We had feelings. We were very different from them. We had preferences that should have been respected. But they weren't.

I remember my mom even making me play in dirt when she realized I did not like it. From a young age, I never liked getting dirty. I was prissy then and still am now. Instead of respecting this, she picked me up, grabbed my hands, and would make me put my hands in the dirt as she yelled, "it's just dirt."

Situations like this made us clash. We were like oil and water. I felt like there was a nicer way to do things. So when clashes happened, it brought out my sassy personality. I honestly couldn't help it either. I naturally had a little extra spunk for my age. A little bit more attitude than other young girls. This was how I was wired to be. It drove her crazy!

The clashes and differences I experienced with my new family made me want to be back at my grandma and grandpa's even more. I even told my mom that I wanted to see my grandma again. I missed her, even though I hadn't been the closest with her when we lived with them. And I started to miss the big boxes of presents they used to send us in the mail. I missed the phone calls that suddenly stopped abruptly.

Me asking to see my grandma didn't sit well with my mom. As soon as I asked, I remember my mom grabbing my shoulders and holding me by them as she told me we were never going to see her again. My mom's face was red. She was extremely upset to the point that it scared me. In that moment, I couldn't understand why I'd never see my grandparents again. I didn't understand why my mom was so mad that I wanted to see them.

Looking back now, it appears as if she had been jealous. That's the only thing that I can think of to explain what was wrong with me wanting to see my grandma and my grandpa. Because of my mom's reaction, I knew to never ask to see them again.

CHAPTER 3:
LEGALLY THEIRS

Our new family was very religious. They were devout Mormons, who went to church every Sunday, and a couple of times throughout the week. Going to church became so much a part of my life with them that it got to the point that I didn't know any different. On Sunday mornings there was never a question about what we would do. We got ready for church and went for a couple of hours that felt like all day.

Just like my parents were devoted to going to church frequently, they were just as devoted to upholding and following all of the restrictions imposed by this religion. For example, they allowed what was taught to dictate what we could and couldn't eat. As well as the clothes we placed on our bodies.

Even though the church we went to was strict and pretty small, some things about it were enjoyable to me. To my surprise, I actually enjoyed learning the songs. So much so that I can still remember some of them to this day. This is most likely because we always sang the same couple of songs before we went to our classes.

In the midst of getting acclimated to our new environment, the adoption process became final. I remember we were given the choice to change our names. During that time it was weird. I played around with many different names. At one moment I wanted to be named Princess Diana because no one could tell me I wasn't a princess. While other times, I changed my name to something else. We literally would go to school every other week with different names. Ultimately, I decided that I was going to keep my first name while my parents chose my middle and last name.

After picking our names, everything was made legal. We now belonged to them for the rest of our lives. We were their children. Their names were on our birth certificates.

Surprisingly, after we got adopted, things changed for us. they started calling me Tachi, Tosh, and even Toe-cheese. I was only called Tachianna when I got into trouble. It was as if Tachianna was now the bad girl. This caused me to hate my name for a large part of my life. I now identified my first name being called with trouble.

I really don't believe that they understood how they made me feel. Or maybe they did, and didn't care. Thankfully, it doesn't matter now because I just started taking back ownership of my name. Now, when people ask me my name, I say it loud and proud: "Tachianna." When asked if I have a nickname, my reply is always, "no."

The way I was addressed was not the only surprising change which occurred after being adopted. We started to now get spanked by our adoptive mother. Bad spankings at times too. I recall one of our teachers asking the kids in our second and third grade mixed class how our home life was. I sat in my chair with my head hung down, swinging my feet back and forth as I told her my mom hit us. As I spoke, the teacher just kind of looked at me. She didn't say anything in response. So I went about my day, like nothing had been said.

That evening, as we were all sitting at the table, the phone rang. By the sound of things, I could tell my mom was talking to my teacher. I quickly became very nervous as she sat in the pantry talking for what seemed like forever. After she hung up the phone, she came back to the table and asked if I wanted to go back to foster care. According to her, it could happen. I instantly thought "yes", but I knew better to not say it out loud.

I couldn't believe my mother acted like she didn't abuse us. You should have seen the look of disgust on her face at the dinner table that night. It was ridiculous! She, as well as my brothers, knew I wasn't lying. We all knew that when they just had legal custody, they didn't spank us. They knew then they weren't allowed to hit or spank us. However, now that we were legally theirs, she abused and punished us often, and out of nowhere. I don't know why I was painted out to be a liar. I had no reason to lie about her.

The next day, I went back to school and acted like nothing had ever happened. The teacher just pretty much acted as if it were no big deal. She acted as if she believed whatever my mother told her. From that day forward, the teacher never asked me anything else. And I stopped liking that teacher.

It appeared as if she, and no one else, wanted to see the truth. All people saw was a family who rescued us. They never asked what was going on. Because of this, they never knew what was going on behind closed doors. In their eyes, my mother was a saint. When in actuality, she was the opposite.

After the school incident, my mother decided it was best that we were homeschooled. I believe the scare of being discovered as a child abuser, and the fact that we started to talk about evolution at school, gave her the excuse she needed. Once we began homeschooling, it took a while before our educational material came. Instead of creating educational things for us to do in the meantime, my mom made us do chores. We were responsible for taking care of the animals, cleaning the bathrooms, doing the dishes, picking weeds, feeding the chickens, caring for and feeding the dogs. We did this all while my mom kind of sat there and "supervised" us.

The only incentive we had at this time was being able to play outside all day. So instead of taking our sweet time, we literally hurried through our chores.

Once all our school stuff came in, we sat at the table together doing our own lessons. We did this while my mom sat at the other end of the table holding a spoon. She would reach over and hit either the top of our heads or hands with it. Or call us over to her, and have us bend over in front of her and hit us.

My mom ran a tight schedule during that time. We did schoolwork. We were only able to get up to use the restroom. And we were allowed to have recess.

I remember how we used to get up early every morning and make sure everything was done by a certain time. Just so that we could make it to the table on time to do things all over again.

Even though she kept this schedule, we were able to breathe a little. She allowed us to watch movies about history and science. In fact, we often watched Bill Nye, Magic School Bus, and School House Rock.

Homeschooling was kind of fun in the beginning. Until there were a lot of days when we just kind of stopped doing schoolwork altogether. As kids, we didn't care because we were able to play instead—all while our books sat at the table.

When school became less of a priority to us, that's when house and field work took its place again. We literally worked in the garden all day. We canned fruit and vegetables. When we were not working in the garden, we learned hands-on how to take care of a home.

We cleaned all the time. Everything had to be cleaned perfectly (I am still very particular about the way that I clean now). At times, when things weren't cleaned the right way, we had to stay up all night cleaning—no exaggeration. Sometimes we were up until 2 in the morning doing dishes, scrubbing, and mopping the floors. We would then be woken up by my mom at 6 am to read scriptures while being half asleep.

There always seemed to be yelling and screaming centered around cleaning. There was so much rage displayed as well. We literally spent most of the time scrubbing walls and baseboards, and cleaning bathrooms 10 times over because there was a spot or strand of hair we could never see. We were even grabbed by the back of our necks as she screamed and pointed at some invisible dirt. Instead of arguing with her, we would clean again as we cried while scrubbing comet off of the bathroom shower, or whatever else the invisible spot or dirt had been. I remember crying sometimes thinking, "I don't see what you see, but I'm just going to clean it anyways." Because of this, from a very young age, I felt like we had no sense of freedom. I was just a little slave cleaning these white peoples' house.

Whenever we failed to meet the expectations set before us, we were punished. But not like other kids. Our punishments were weird. For instance, I remember my brother had purposely gotten locked outside of the house one night. Because all of the sheds and cars were locked, he had no choice but to sleep underneath the car. He had no food, or blanket to keep him warm. I talked to him through the window for a little while to keep him company, but after that, he had no company either. He slept underneath the car like an animal, all while my parents slept soundly. I still can't understand how anybody could just go to sleep knowing they locked out their child. Or how anyone could justify why it was okay to do this to any human being, let alone a child.

When my brother finally came in the next morning, he didn't talk to anybody. His eyes were visibly swollen from crying. As he walked past us, he put his head down and went straight to his bedroom. I can only imagine the humiliation he must have felt that morning after being treated like a dog! In my parents' minds, were we really lower than the animals? If not, it felt like we were.

I don't know what was better, playing outside all day, even though I hated it, or being in the house with her. I know that may sound weird because what kid our ages didn't like playing outside. But it was because there were times when our mom would force us to stay outside all day. During those times, to satisfy our thirst, we would drink from the yard hose. On the occasions she gave us food to eat, she would come to the back porch and hand us peanut butter and jelly sandwiches, along with some kind of fruit. And there were days we weren't allowed to eat, as a form of punishment because of something we did. To help us get through the days where we weren't fed, we would pretend that we were Native Americans. On those days, we would go to the garden and pick stuff, chop it all up, and eat it. Or we would put it in a bell pepper like a bowl.

CHAPTER 4: IRON FIST

We grew up with an iron fist to say the least. The forms of punishment that we suffered were severe and almost always carried out at the hands of our mother. This was because she didn't work and was always home. My dad was always gone at work, at church, working in the yard, or doing side jobs (I enjoyed his side jobs because he would sometimes take us with him).

My dad was different from my mom. He was funny and nice. On his days off, he spent time with us making breakfast. Those days were my favorite because we had stakes of toast and hot chocolate and crepes (my dad made the best crepes) filled with sugar and fruit.

Back then, my dad was oblivious to a lot of things. I believe this was because his main focus was working to provide for our family, even if it meant working all of the time—regardless of the fact that he had a lot of pain in his back and down in his legs from surgeries and cancer. He worked a lot to provide. Even though he had to walk with a limp and a little hunched over, he still worked without making any excuses. He just got the job done, and for that I admire him greatly.

Sometimes I wonder how things would have been different if he hadn't worked so much. Would he have protected us? Would he have allowed my mom to be so hard on us? I'm sad to say, the circumstances would mostly have been the same. Why? because there had been others in my family that overlooked the abuse.

There had been times while being at my other grandma's house, my mom would mistreat us. I recall instances when we were over at her house for a family reunion or Sunday dinner. People were playing cards and things like that. My mom would sit there and tell them we couldn't eat while everybody else ate whatever my grandma cooked. To justify this, she'd tell them it was because we did something, or we didn't feed an animal. During those times, I remember starving while everyone else ate in front of us, as I wondered why anybody didn't tell her that it was wrong. Why didn't anyone hand us a plate?

Denying us food wasn't the only thing she did in front of them either. Sometimes she hit us in front of them. Even though they saw, nobody stood up for us. Because they did nothing to protect us as children, as I got older it made me mad, and I distanced myself from them. This meant that I no longer went to family reunions or Sunday dinners. Distance was better because they failed to have my back as a child. Nobody did the one thing I wanted most: for somebody to save us . . . for somebody to love us . . . for somebody to take us away. But I knew that couldn't have happened because my mom had painted us out to be these bad kids, which made me feel like the black sheep of the family.

Because no one stood up for us, we experienced several different kinds of abuse at her hands. Honestly, I feel like the abuse we suffered was so severe because my mother was an angry person. She got mad at any little thing that we did. Once that happened, she was a different person. She would go from being calm and composed, to having a bright red face as she loudly yelled while spitting everywhere. This made me truly scared of her, because no matter how hard we tried to do right, nothing we did was ever right.

We literally got hit, or punished in some form, every single day; most of the time, multiple times a day. I'm not saying that giving your child a spanking is wrong, or that taking away something as a form of discipline is wrong. I'm a firm believer in discipline. What we experienced was beyond acceptable discipline. It was Pure Evil.

My mom hit us with fly swatters (which I honestly believe was her favorite form of abuse to inflict on us). Most of the time, it was never just one hit (and if it was, I was very shocked, to say the least). My mom would hit us repeatedly after she uttered, "bend down and grab your ankles." These words were what I hated hearing—not only as they were being said to me, but as I watched the person before me jumping up and down rubbing their butts as we were all lined up waiting for our turn to endure the same spanking.

Since we wouldn't remain in the position she requested, we got hit just about everywhere. My mom would hit our ankles, our fingers, our heads, backs, legs, and anywhere else. All while insisting that it was our fault for not bending down and grabbing our ankles.

One night, I remember having welts all over my body. There were these two lines with a little oval down the middle and the sides of my body that were raised. I just lay there on my stomach because my back, butt, and legs were all welted. I remember us all lying on the bunk beds quietly with marks all over our bodies. Sometimes the welts lasted a couple of days.

Once, we were brave enough to tell her about the marks remaining on our bodies. We even went as far as bending over to show her. To our surprise, she sat there in denial. She sat there with a lack of empathy towards us. She sat there with no compassion towards us for what she had done. Her reaction was both unbelievable and horrible.

What was even more horrible was her response towards me when she realized that she had spanked me for something I had not done. That particular time there was some mix up about homework. She beat me so that I had really bad welts all the way down my legs and on my butt. Instead of admitting she had been wrong, she took me shopping. On the car ride to the store, I could barely sit in the car because it hurt really bad. The entire ride, I sat trying to adjust myself back and forth off of my welts to minimize the pain. Once at the store, she gave me some dresses to try on and looked me dead in my face and said, "don't take your pants off."

I remember sitting in the dressing room wanting to walk out with my bare legs but couldn't. Pulling down my pants hurt my body. Sitting hurt. Standing hurt. My body was in so much pain at that moment that I wanted people to see my legs. I wanted her to get in trouble. Despite the pain I would feel, I contemplated whether or not I should do it. Ultimately, I decided against it.

Looking back now, deciding to not tell anyone outside of my family about the abuse we suffered, resulted in more abuse up until I was around 14 years old. Until that time, my mom would place us on her lap and bend us over and hit us repeatedly as the others were lined up waiting for their turn. We jumped around the kitchen crying, screaming, rubbing our butts, while repeatedly saying, "no, no, no, we're sorry." When she was really upset, she would pull out a drawer for us to put our head under so that we wouldn't move around as she held our t-shirt. We were being held as if we had on dog collars as we spun in circles getting hit in the kitchen. It was a heartbreaking scene for sure. As one child got hit, the other lay on the floor crying and screaming loudly. At one point, so many spoons had been broken over one of our foster brothers, I thought she was going to kill him! She even said that he had to go because she was going to hurt him.

When we weren't getting hit with spoons, my mom was either flicking our ears or slapping us in the face—sometimes both at the same time, red faced, screaming, yelling, or even biting her bottom lip. She did this until the brown skin on my ears became red, causing my ears to hurt for days at a time. Just like with the flicking of the ears, she would smack me in the face, either once, or on both sides of my face—when she was really mad, repeatedly with both of her hands. I just wanted to cock back and slap her back one time. I even grabbed her t-shirt and pushed her. That day I was fed up with getting hit!

My mother's rage was unpredictable to say the least. It caused her to make us run laps without shoes where there were goat's head and weeds everywhere. She made us stand in the corner for half the day; sometimes with our hands up until they were weak.

Anything we loved, she would take away as a form of punishment; so I learned to not love anything. And if that wasn't enough, we were called stupid, talked about to family members in our presence, and told we had issues learning because we had fetal alcohol syndrome.

When we were not being hit, we were being forced to eat things, or denied food as a form of punishment. My mother would force us to eat things that we absolutely hated. I have always been very sensitive to different textures on my tongue. As a result, I didn't like feeling certain foods in my mouth. Eggs was one of those foods. Even though she knew that I hated eggs, she would continuously make me eat them. I literally would gag and run to the bathroom and throw up after eating them. One morning, while we were still going to regular school, she made me stay back and sit at the table and eat the eggs she had prepared for breakfast. That morning, I tried everything in my power not to eat them, including dunking my chocolate milk in them. But my mom didn't care. I had to still eat them.

Finally, after sitting at the table for hours, I gave in and started to eat the eggs as she watched. As I placed the cold chocolate covered eggs in my mouth, I gagged repeatedly. I did this as I threw up in my mouth. Once I finished, I had to walk a couple of miles to school as she drove on the side of me in the van.

The times we had been denied food was when we forgot to feed the dog or chickens. She would make us go all day with no food, or no water, because she was teaching us a lesson. After a while, I started stealing food when she refused to feed us. I stole bread and lunch meat by hiding it under my shirt. I would run into the bathroom and eat it as quickly as I could. After being successful at stealing food, I was no longer going to starve. I was no longer going to accept "no" where eating was concerned. I was no longer going to be hungry; I was going to take what I wanted!

CHAPTER 5: SCARRED BY VERBAL ABUSE

Being verbally put down by my mom was so commonplace that I didn't even know that there was such a thing as verbal abuse until I got older. We were called stupid and idiot literally every day of our whole life. Being verbally abused all the time does something to you. It does something to your brain. When you hear certain things that much, it's like a light switch is turned on that causes you to begin to think that it's true.

Growing up, I don't ever remember being told anything positive from my mom. It was always, "you can't do this; you can't do that; you aren't smart enough to do that." Or, "they have so much trouble learning because they have fetal alcohol syndrome." And being told that everything I did I couldn't do because something was wrong with me.

She literally had whole conversations with different family members about how we just aren't smart. I sat there frustrated because you would have thought that the classes that she took to become a foster parent would have taught her the effects that verbal abuse would have on children. I couldn't understand why she didn't know that it wasn't right to talk to us, or about us, the way she did. I couldn't understand why she couldn't encourage us; or why she didn't bless us and build us up by telling us that regardless of what we have been born with, we can do anything we set our minds to; or why she didn't tell us that we are smart.

Because I truly believed that I was stupid and an idiot, I started to lash out towards her. I was so fed up! Whenever she kept asking why I didn't do something, I wanted to look her in the face and tell her "because I'm stupid remember." No matter how bad I wanted to say it, I wasn't bold enough. I didn't have it in me.

But one day my brother did. My brother's boldness didn't stop there. One time while on a family camping trip, my brother went to drink out of a jug. My mom screamed from across the campground, "get your nigger lips off that jug." As she said it, her face was the same bright red it had been on those occasions when she was really upset while whooping us. I knew, just like then, that she meant what she had said. No one could believe she uttered the words, including my dad. He was visibly disappointed.

Instead of apologizing, my mother made a thousand excuses as to why she had said it. One excuse was that she grew up hearing that word. I didn't believe that was the reason why she had said it. I felt that her true colors were showing as she finally expressed how she really felt about us—we were just a bunch of stupid niggers to her.

That day my brother ran away for hours in the forest. When he came back, he wasn't the same anymore. That's the day my brother just stopped caring, and really started doing whatever he wanted. Looking back, I don't blame him. He had lost all respect for her, and it was her fault.

The fact that we didn't know something, or were stupid as she put it, wasn't our fault. It wasn't even our biological mother's fault either. It was hers. She was the one who was supposed to homeschool us. She was the one who was supposed to teach us. Instead, she put us down whenever we were actually being homeschooled, instead doing chores around the house. I remember whenever we didn't know the answer to something, instead of her explaining it, she called us stupid.

When calling me stupid didn't make me answer correctly, she put me over the deep freezer with a timer next to me. Whenever it went off, which was every couple of minutes, and I couldn't do the worksheet that she wanted me to do, she would scream as she hit me. She repeated this as if it were going to help, but it didn't. It only traumatized me. I would sit in fear of getting hit, all while blaming myself because "you're stupid." "You're stupid" rung in my ears. I sat there in a panic as I waited for the timer to go off, and the cycle of her screaming and hitting me would start over again, followed by her setting the timer again.

Being in constant fear and panic, I couldn't even focus on the schoolwork. The schoolwork was always hard for me. I didn't know the answer because my teacher, which was her, didn't teach me like she was supposed to. As she degraded me, I felt like an animal. As a result of the traumatization, I became numb to it all.

Being constantly told I was stupid, or an idiot, as a child scarred me. I hesitated with so many things in life. Those words caused me to not achieve goals because I thought I wasn't smart enough to do it.

Those words made me feel awkward having conversation with people. I constantly kept thinking that they too would see that I was a stupid fetal alcohol child. I felt they too would agree with my mom that I was a person incapable of learning because my birth mother drank alcohol when she was carrying me.

I just wanted to be loved by her. I just wanted her to pick us up and love us. But she wasn't built like that. Growing up I always thought she was incapable of showing love towards us because we weren't her biological children. I grew to think that being abused, instead of loved and being shown love, was how it was supposed to be when you lived in a foster home—that it was normal to be rejected and hated. Looking back now, I know that these feelings caused me to hate everybody. What I experienced caused me to become so jealous of other people.

When other mothers showed the love that I wanted towards their daughters, I was jealous. I couldn't understand why I was getting spanked, yelled at, and even touched! I just couldn't understand what made me so unlovable.

I really started to hate my life. I hated that I was born. But I kept all of these feelings bottled up and hidden from others. I pretended that I was happy. When I was really angry.

CHAPTER 6: **MOLESTATION**

I never even knew that "molestation" was the proper term to use for what I experienced. Mainly because it was done by another child who had been a couple of years older than me. Whenever I wasn't being physically and emotionally abused by my mother, I was being touched every day. Sometimes even multiple times a day for a very long time. As normal as it had become, I knew it wasn't normal. But it was *my normal*. Who was I going to tell? Who was going to believe me? I was called a liar for things I never lied about. Yes, there were times that I had lied as a child. Especially when I would get hit no matter what I said. So I lied at times because I was trying to get the least amount of spankings possible.

The molestation started when a big box of porn was found by the other child by the house next door. But I can't blame it completely on that because I feel as though it would have happened anyways. Before I go into detail about what did happen, I must tell you this, I do not hate the other child. Yes, I was angry for many years. During that time, I did not talk to him. I was only able to move towards forgiving him for what he had done because I opened up about it when I went to see a therapist. She was the first person who told me that a lot of boys are touched, and they never talk about it.

After hearing this, I wrote the other child a very detailed descriptive letter on social media detailing what he had done to me. To my surprise, he responded with a very heartfelt message. Not only did he tell me he was sorry, but he revealed that he had been touched by a girl, maybe a babysitter, when he was younger. As a result, he thought it was something normal.

All I could think about while reading his response was that I finally had the proof that I needed. I went straight to my mom to show it to her. I was very scared. Even though it crushed me to show her the two very long messages we had sent to each other, I did it anyway. After reading the messages, she handed me back the phone. She told me I pretty much lied so much as a kid she didn't know what to believe. She cried though. Not because he had touched me, but because he had been touched. All I could think was, "what about me? what about the things I had gone through?" All I could think about was this is the reason why I blamed her for it happening more when I got older. I felt as though she had just written it all off.

What happened to me was very real and traumatizing. It turned me into a sexual monster. I was around 7 or 8 years old when it first started. I know this to be the case because in the Mormon religion you are baptized when you're 8 years old. I cannot remember the very first time it happened because I've blocked a lot of stuff out. But I know that it started while we were playing house. He would cry like a baby and lay in my lap and tell me he was hungry. At that time, I didn't have boobs, but that didn't stop him from "feeding." I remember him sucking on my nipples as I rubbed his hair. I didn't think anything of it because we were playing house and that's something moms did when they would feed their baby.

In the beginning, it was very touchy feely. There was kissing and petting. He was always sneaking around trying to touch me.

I became very sexualized because of the early onset of sexual molestation. When my mom would leave me home alone, I would go into her bedroom and put on her makeup because I wanted to be sexy. I watched shows like Jerry Springer where the women wore short skirts with red lipstick and big hair. I don't know if it was because of the porn magazines and what was going on, but I was drawn to that. So when my mom would leave, I went into her bedroom and put on her makeup and this one silky piece of lingerie that she had hid in the back of her closet.

Although I was acting in this manner, I finally got tired of what was going on with the other child. I would beg my mother to take me with her instead of leaving me home when he was around. She would allow me to go. I wasn't even concerned about what we were getting, or how long it would take us. I felt more safe going with my mom grocery shopping, even though the car ride was boring. It was better than being left at home when he was around!

Unfortunately, my safety was shattered when she started leaving me at home again. After that, things seemed to be getting worse. He became more aggressive towards me. Once, while I was in the bathroom located near the kitchen, he caused me to fall and break the towel rack when he was trying to touch me inappropriately. When my mom asked who broke it, he instantly told her it was me, so she spanked me.

In that moment, I wanted to tell her everything. But I didn't. She wouldn't have believed me. Her only concern then was the broken towel rack. Not the reason behind why, or how, it had gotten broken.

That incident didn't stop or slow him down. After that, we were playing in the fort outside when he asked me to taste him. He wanted to see how far I could put it in my mouth. I did it, and immediately started to gag. It was nasty.

During the summertime, my parents would allow us children that were at the house to sleep outside, in either our huge family tent, or on the trampoline. Whether we were in it, or on the trampoline, I would fall asleep next to my brother. Somehow, the other child would always end up by me.

One of those nights, I woke up to him on the top of me. I remember laying there with my nightgown up worried. I told him that I didn't want to get pregnant (even though it wasn't possible because I was too young), but I continued to lay there as he moved in and out. To deal with what was happening, I told myself that we were playing house. This is what moms and dads did.

After that night, he wanted more. When he came around, he would look at the porn magazines and try the different positions he saw in them. He became really bold. He would touch me at all times. It could be broad daylight, but a lot in the middle of the night. He told me that if we were to get caught, to say he was beating me up.

One day, my mom walked in on us. As soon as she walked in, he rolled off of me slowly. She asked us what we were doing. Instead of telling the truth, I told her he was beating me up. I didn't want to get in trouble. She must have known something else was going on because she questioned us separately and then again together. I continued to stick with my answer that he was beating me up. I know deep down she knew.

It was not the first time we had been close to getting caught. It wasn't the last time either. She questioned us a couple of more times. But nothing ever came of it, so she left it alone. My mom had always been the one in denial about things. Even though he would make up stupid obvious lies, like "I was rolling over her" or "you know I sag my pants, they fell down." I hated her for believing him.

The sexual abuse continued to occur for four years. It stopped around the time when there were two female foster kids living with us. One of the girls was a little older than me, and the other was a little younger than I was. The other child stopped abusing me because he started to mess around with the older one. They would be in the fort together and I was not allowed to go in. I knew what was happening inside of there.

The girls eventually decided to tell their social worker about the other child touching them and about my mother hitting us. I remember we were in the van driving with my mom. She had gotten a call from the girls' social worker. My mother told us what the social worker had said. She even told the other child that they wanted to give him a lie detector test. He looked so scared. I said real sassy, "yeah, do it." I wanted him to get in trouble.

He didn't have to take a lie detector test. The social worker removed the girls from our home instead. No one asked me what happened. No one removed me or my brothers. I was left there for the abuse to continue. Now that I am an adult, I get angry at the system. I just wanted somebody to protect me.

After this, my mom was allowed to still care for foster children. But she opted to not take in any more girls, unless they were babies.

Over time, I became immune to what happened between the other child and I. Things seemed to get a little easier. It became easier for me to perform oral sex on him than it was for me to have sex with him.

The first time my cherry had been popped I was 14 years old. It was in our kitchen. He had put his penis inside of me. As he pushed really hard, I screamed as blood came out. I was freaked out because my blood was all over the kitchen floor. We had already been having sex for years by this time, but for whatever reason, it hadn't popped until that moment.

By the time I was 15 years old, I found myself wanting it. He would wrap saran wrap around his penis because he didn't have condoms. When we didn't have any saran wrap, he used his P.E. shorts which I hated because it hurt really bad.

This continued until one day I looked at him and told him, "don't you ever touch me again." To my surprise he didn't. It was that simple. I became angry with myself. I started to question myself as to why I hadn't said that before that moment.

I started to blame myself. I never put up a fight. I always just let things happen. Whenever I think about what happened for all those years, I become disgusted. Did I want that to happen? Did I really enjoy it because I never fought? I never kicked and screamed or said no.

Thoughts like this always left me feeling guilty, perverted, and nasty. I often wondered how I would have been if it never happened to me. What happened to me for all of those years resulted in me turning into such a sexual person. It's so weird. I felt like if sexual things weren't being done to me, something was wrong. I had become so attached to my own perpetrator. I grew accustomed to the abuse. It was my norm.

I know it sounds sick. It's something that I don't even really want to talk about. It's something that I'm embarrassed about. But the undeniable truth is that what happened to me for over an 8-year period of time, really messed with me mentally. It opened the door up for me to become a sexual monster.

I slept around because of what happened to me. I hated when people called me a slut; they didn't understand that promiscuity was literally embedded into my brain. The spirit of lust had been placed over my little body at such a young age.

As horrible as the sexual abuse was, I forgave the other child. What happened in the past is now in the past. He would literally give me the shirt off of his back. He has done many things for me as an adult. I don't know if it's guilt, or shame. The truth is this, I don't think he is an evil person anymore. I don't think that he would harm anyone. I didn't write this about him to hurt him. It wasn't to get revenge. But it's to tell my story.

CHAPTER 7: TEENAGE YEARS

As a teenager, I suffered from low self-esteem and low self-worth. I never felt pretty. I really thought I was ugly growing up around predominantly white people. I didn't have long hair down to my butt like the other girls. My skin was hyperpigmented (and still is to this day). I hated the scars on my face. I hated that I wasn't athletic like the other girls in the church around me.

I saw that everyone around me wanted blondes. I clearly wasn't a blonde. This made me feel insecure. I felt as though I was not good enough.

I hated the skin that I was in. We were treated differently by everyone. Not only were we the black kids, but a lot of people had more money than we had, and they made sure to treat us like it.

I hated it. I just wanted to fit in in a town where there wasn't a lot of minorities. I did not fit in, no matter how much I wanted to. I stuck out, even with the minorities. They told me I was too white. I never understood what they meant; my skin looked just like theirs. I know that I didn't speak like them, which they made fun of. I didn't have braids like they had. I had never owned a pair of Nikes until I was about 20 years old.

I was bullied, made fun of, and hated, instead of being accepted. I was made fun of because of my hair. They would ask me if I had been wearing a wig. A girl even pulled my hair extremely hard one time because she didn't believe it was my real hair. I acted as if it didn't hurt, when in fact it hurt for a couple of days.

These feelings, coupled with the fact that I had been sexualized at such a young age, caused me to become sexually active at a young age. I felt like I had to have sex with every boyfriend, or they wouldn't like me. What's sad is that some of them didn't even know what sex was until they met me. I may have ruined a lot of boys' lives because they possibly would have waited longer if it weren't for me. At the time of each encounter, I didn't feel this way. But I felt so guilty about it later on in life.

The second person I ever had sex with was on another tile floor. It was different from the previous times with the other child. I was tense. I didn't want him to kiss me. I felt kind of gross. Instead of enjoying the moment, I lay on that tile floor looking at the ceiling, as he went in and out of me. The encounter ended pretty quickly when his dad knocked on the bathroom door. He broke up with me right after that. Followed by him telling everybody at school that we had sex.

The next time I had sex was in a convenience store restroom right by my school. Just like with the guy before, he told everybody. Instead of being concerned, I didn't even care. I thought this is what every girl was doing. In my mind, this is what they wanted from me. I honestly couldn't understand why they were going around telling everybody.

This was because I wasn't prepared for the real world. Being homeschooled for all of those years resulted in me being sheltered. In my naive mind, I believed that they were supposed to be keeping us a secret. They weren't supposed to tell anyone. I really thought that they would keep their mouths shut just like the other child and I had. Because they didn't, everybody at school questioned me about what had been said. Instead of telling them the truth, I did what I had done in the past, I denied everything. I told all who asked that they had lied.

Back then, I couldn't understand why they would tell our secret. I felt like it wasn't anyone else's business. I had kept a secret my whole life! I couldn't understand why they couldn't do the same.

Having sex wasn't that big of deal to me. I literally was doing something sexual all the time.

My sexual encounters and sexual behavior halted shortly after my 8th grade year. My mother decided I, along with my biological brother, would be homeschooled. My other brother was allowed to go to school because my mother felt like he was smarter than we were. I felt this wasn't fair. I was disappointed to say the least. I knew that I would not be homeschooled, rather I would go back to taking care of the house and my younger siblings.

During my teenage years, I was always like a mom to my other younger siblings. Despite the fact that there had been two foster kids removed from our home, they kept allowing my parents to foster more. Kids were constantly always coming in and out of our home my whole life. And my mom had two miracle children.

Because of this, I was never allowed to be a teenager. I wasn't really allowed to hang out with the few friends I did have. And the ones I did have, were friends from church. We would only hang out when we went to church stuff like dances, or to youth activities during the week. Even though this was the case, I never felt truly connected to them.

I was never allowed to be a kid like they were. I always had to help babysit, clean, and cook. Unlike them, I couldn't go walking around the mall with my friends. Or do anything else that they were allowed to do. I never had that sense of freedom. This made me jealous and envious of them. They were allowed to have parties. They got to wear whatever they wanted, while I hated the clothes my mom bought me. They were close to their mothers like I wanted to be to mine.

CHAPTER 8: **FREE AT LAST**

Being homeschooled was not for me. My parents kept telling me to do my schoolwork. To appease them, I would sit down and stare at the assignments. When I did complete something, I used a cheat sheet to do it. I did not know how to do the work. I couldn't comprehend what I was reading most of the time. And it wasn't my fault. When I was younger being homeschooled, I wasn't taught much, besides how to keep a house.

Oftentimes, when I attempted to complete my schoolwork, I became frustrated. During those times I thought about how much I would rather work instead. Aside from them telling me to do my work, my parents never taught us the importance of going to school. They never explained the importance of needing a high school diploma. And talks about college were out of the question. Work was glorified in my home. As a result, all I wanted to do was get a job and make my own money, so that I could move out of the house.

When I was 16 years old, I finally gained a little bit of freedom. I was allowed to start working my first job, which was at a pizza place. I was beyond excited. For the first time in my life, I was able to make my own money! It didn't stop there either. I then got a job at a daycare center, followed by a fast food place. Because I worked with a lot of Hispanic people, I even started to pick up on speaking Spanish.

Even though I liked working at the fast food place, I knew that I didn't get the job based off of skills. Rather, my boss thought that I was cute. So he decided to hire me. He made it known too. He constantly said different things to me. He was always flirting with me. I was disgusted. He was a short little fat man.

There I was 16 years old, getting sexually harassed by a grown man. He invited me to the bar a couple of times. It was unbelievable. Everyone, co-workers included, could tell that he had a crush on me. Instead of saying anything about it, I used his attraction to me to my benefit. I went along with the flirting to get extra hours. The more hours I worked meant that I would get off at night. That meant that I didn't have to go home and do homework.

When I wasn't working nights, I took advantage of getting off early. Instead of going straight home, I would get off and go hangout with one of the guys I had been dating from the church. Which didn't go all too well because I had a pregnancy scare with one of them.

There I was 16 years old, having to tell my mother that I might be pregnant. She was disappointed. She insisted that I was going to have to marry the guy if I was. I was appalled. I couldn't understand why I would have to marry someone when I was only 16 years old. Thankfully, I found out when I went to the gynecologist that I wasn't pregnant after all. I was relieved, and so was she. Needless to say, my mom made me breakup with that guy.

After the pregnancy scare, I became more focused on working and less about completing any schoolwork. I figured that I would either just work until the day I died, or I would get married and be taken care of.

I enjoyed being at work. Things were different there. Being there actually helped me to get over being socially awkward. Prior to working, I had always felt socially awkward around people. I struggled to have simple conversations. This was because I really didn't know what to say. I was always scared to really say anything because I was scared that people were going to judge me. I didn't want them to think that I was stupid.

Fortunately for me, my fears never became reality. I felt safe at work. People generally asked me how I was. They helped me to lighten up a lot. For the first time, I had people around me that cared and helped me to genuinely laugh. This was a different experience for me.

I managed to work my way up to a lead position. I was proud of myself. I now had more money than I had ever had in my life. Because I wasn't taught the value of money, I didn't know how to save it, or what to do with it. As crazy as it sounds, I didn't even know how to pay bills. So I got my paycheck and blew it.

With this newfound freedom came a confidence that I didn't have before. Yes, before this point, my boss had thought I was cute and I had boyfriends, but I still did things because I wanted to feel wanted and pretty.

Something happened once I started working and making my own money. I started to realize that I was actually pretty. People would flirt with me all of the time. While I was working the drive-thru, I had regular customers, some of which were older men, who would specifically ask for me. They would even give me their numbers. I had never received attention like that in my entire life. Being told that I was beautiful boosted my confidence. So much so that I would flirt right back. I made sure that I always went to work with makeup on and my hair done. I started to crave attention!

The customers weren't the only one whose attention I had. Apparently, I had the attention of one of my co-workers too, Greg. He worked the night shift after he got out of school, while I worked the day shift. Sometimes, when they needed to change my schedule, I would work with him. The entire time we worked together, he was always extremely nice to me. He would always smile at me and offer to do a lot of my job for me. It was kind of nice. He would literally cook, bag the food, and hand it out of the window to the waiting customer. Greg did triple the work just to impress me. It didn't stop there either. Greg made it a point to show me his super clean gold Toyota Camry.

I liked the attention he gave me. I often flirted back with him. We would flirt so much, while always trying to take our breaks at the same time, that everybody there knew that we liked each other. They even encouraged us to start dating. So we did.

I quickly learned that Greg was a lot different from me in more ways than one. For starters, he was still a virgin. I was shocked! I thought, "how are you a senior in high school and a virgin?" But he was. Then he told me he didn't like Mormons and he didn't believe in God. I should have run away right then, but I didn't. I paid more attention to the way that he treated me.

Aside from the flirting, he treated me well. We became close very quickly. I even opened up to him about me not liking my home life that much. He was somebody nice to talk to. Somebody who cared about me for me and not for my body.

Eventually, I did something that I had never done with anyone else, I took him to meet my parents. It was pretty awkward to say the least. I don't think they were very fond of him. He was a little bit older and had a car. But I didn't care.

After that, I started hanging out with him even more. Whenever he wasn't giving me rides to the places I needed to go, I would go with him to hang out with his friends, or with his little brother. It was different being around them. They spoke in Spanish most of the time. Because I didn't know as much Spanish as they did, he was always translating back and forth to me. I enjoyed spending time with him.

CHAPTER 9: **WHEN TRAGEDY STRIKES**

Greg, his brother, and I also worked together at the fast food restaurant. But we didn't always work the same shift. You would have thought that because we spent so much time together, his brother would appreciate the time he had free from being around us. For whatever reason he didn't.

One night, Greg and I were scheduled for closing. His brother decided that he wanted to be annoying. He came through the drive through yelling through the intercom. Initially, I didn't know it was him. As he yelled, I yelled back through the headsets. Once he came to the window, we realized that it had been him the entire time.

Greg was not amused by his behavior one bit. He told his brother to go home. Greg's brother kept laughing as he said, "bye Greg." Greg told him to stop messing around and to go back to their brother's house. He told him that he would see him when we got off.

Even though he had been annoyed by his younger brother, you could still tell that he loved him a lot. Although they were brothers, Greg was more like the older brother/dad to him. It was visible in this situation. His brother finally left.

After we got off of work, it was extremely late. Even though I had this newfound freedom, I knew that I couldn't hangout that night with them. So Greg took me home. Early the next morning, I received a frantic call from Greg asking me if I had seen his brother. Of course, I had not.

I became worried. I asked my mom to take me to their house. Once there, Greg and I drove all around town searching for his younger brother. We looked everywhere for him and the green car he always drove. We couldn't find him anywhere.

I felt horrible. I tried my best to be there for him. To give him as much moral support as possible. While not really knowing what to say or do. I had never been in this type of situation before.

When we couldn't find him, we went back to their mother's house. By this time, his entire family had arrived. Greg's mom is one of 16 kids, so their family is extremely large to say the least. Once we pulled up, I was extremely heartbroken seeing how devastated they were. They all were crying, screaming, and upset because nobody could find Bobby. To console Greg, I rubbed his back. I did this as I watched everyone crying as they spoke in Spanish to one another.

The scene became more heart wrenching when the car occupied by their three older brothers pulled up. Two of them got out of the car and fell to their knees crying uncontrollably. The look on Greg's mom's face signaled to everyone that Bobby was gone. What happened next is something that I will never forget.

Grown men fell on their knees with snot running down their faces as they cried. All the women started to scream in unison as they all cried out. All the younger cousins were in one room huddled together crying. I stood there in shock. I couldn't believe the night before he was alive, and just like that, he was gone.

The wailing and the screaming was horrific. Everybody was now in different corners of the house crying, as more family and friends arrived. Their mother kept repeating his name over and over again, as if trying to call him back to life. In that moment, I didn't know how to be there for Greg, but I knew I had to stay with him. I didn't want to overstep my boundaries, but I just wanted him to know that I was there if he needed me.

Initially, I didn't know what had happened because everyone there had been speaking in Spanish the entire time. I didn't come to realize why everyone had reacted the way they did until the couple of people who spoke English started to speak. I was shocked to learn that they had found Bobby on top of the hill with two gunshots to his head from an apparent suicide. Inside of his car were alcohol bottles.

After the news broke, I called my mom and told her what had happened. She asked if she needed to come pick me up. I quickly said, no, I needed to be there.

I didn't know that people really killed themselves. From what others had said, Bobby had been suicidal in the past. This time he had succeeded in taking his life over a girl. They were all enraged and wanted to kill her because of it.

I learned for the first time that day that Bobby wasn't the first one in their family to commit suicide. Greg's older brother, who I had never heard of before this point, had hung himself. This was the reason why the family moved to this town. Not only that, but the other brothers at one point or another, were pretty suicidal. I couldn't believe it! I had never seen an entire family devastated and depressed to the point that they wanted to kill themselves.

The death of Bobby had a lasting effect on everyone. His mother was often seen staring out of the back window crying his name as she asked God, "why Bobby?" Greg would sit there holding her as he assured her that everything was going to be okay. This was all too much for me to handle. I wanted to break up with him. But then I would start feeling guilty. In those moments, I felt like I would have been a bad person if I would have broken up with him after his brother's funeral.

Shortly after the funeral, I found out that I was pregnant. I moved in with Greg at his mother's house to be closer to him. At the time that I made this move, I wasn't even 18 years old yet. To my surprise, my mom never tried to come and find me. Yes, she knew exactly where I had worked, but she never came. Instead, she sent one of her friends. On that particular day, her friends drove through the drive-thru of the fast food restaurant and asked me if I was okay. I knew they were only asking because she had sent them, not because they had been concerned themselves.

This bothered me. I felt that if my mom really loved me, if she really had cared for me, she would at the very least show up to my job herself. Or she would have said something before that point. Prior to moving to their house, I had started to pack some of my belongings little by little. It wasn't hard for her to notice that a lot of my stuff was gone, either. Because she never noticed, it made me not care that I was moving out without telling her.

Greg's mother did not care that I had moved into her house. Greg wanted me there with him. He made it clear that he wasn't going to move out. According to him, somebody had to live with her. There was no way that she could be left alone.

There were a lot of people living in that house. His other brother moved in and his girlfriend, who was also pregnant. It was no big deal. It was completely normal for all of us to live there. Everybody helped pay for everything together. I wasn't accustomed to that lifestyle, but I liked the close-knit family that they seemed to have.

I thought it was going to be all fun and games moving in with my boyfriend. Boy, was I wrong! living with a Hispanic mother wasn't that easy. Shortly after I moved in, Greg had gotten a better job working at a welding plant. He had to get up between 3 and 4 o'clock in the morning. His mother would wake me up, telling me to get up and make him some breakfast and to pack his lunch. I was confused as to why I had to do this. I thought to myself, "doesn't he have two arms, can't he do this himself?"

Early on in my pregnancy, I became very sick. It got to the point that I weighed so little that even the doctor thought that I was bulimic. Prior to getting pregnant, I was naturally 115 pounds, and had been skinny my whole life. But with the pregnancy sickness, I couldn't keep anything down. I literally threw up everything at the smell of anything. Everything I tried to eat came right back up.

Greg told me I didn't have to work anymore because I was so sick. This was perfect for me because all I wanted to do was sleep. Because I couldn't keep any food down, I was always exhausted. I had never felt so weak in my entire life. I was always used to working in or outside of the house. Now I could barely lift a finger.

My extreme sickness did not matter to Greg's mother. She pretty much explained to me that it was the woman's job to take care of her husband. This was very difficult for me to understand. I wasn't raised to believe that. Growing up, my dad did everything himself. I understood that I should cook dinner for him, but I just couldn't wrap my head around why I had to pack his lunch. Especially when I was sick, and the smell of food made me sicker.

Instead of saying a word, I didn't. I quickly learned not to argue with a Hispanic mom; it's literally pointless. In their family it was her way, no matter what.

I honestly learned a lot of things from her, even though I had been ungrateful at the time. When she was cooking, I'd be right there in the kitchen with her, learning how to cook their kind of food. During the process, I even learned more Spanish. It got to the point that she would talk to me in Spanish and I understood everything that she said.

As I adjusted to living with Greg's and his family, he suddenly changed from the nice man that I had fallen in love with. He started drinking and crying every day. It may have been because he became very depressed when his brother passed away. I'm not completely certain. I literally watched him turn into a different person in front of my very eyes.

Once he changed, our dynamic changed too. Instead of things being peaceful and loving between us, we started to get into a lot of arguments. I found myself always begging him not to drink because I knew what it would do to him. During this time, his mother would always say that it's my fault that we argued because

I would yell back. No one would admit that he had a drinking problem. Instead, they wanted to place the blame on anybody but him.

Nobody ever thought about getting him some type of counseling. With the passing of Bobby, Greg had become the baby of the family. With that, he was definitely babied by his family. Even though that was the case, I wasn't going to allow him to scream at me during his alcoholic rages.

His family did not like the fact that I stood up for myself. They started to talk about me. They even started to lie on me. This close-knit family environment now turned into a toxic family environment. Their behavior showed me that they were bald faced liars. I couldn't believe it; I was not used to this kind of stuff growing up.

After Greg got a new job, we decided to get a house about 30 minutes away. By this time, I finally told my parents that I was pregnant. Early on, I had decided that I wouldn't tell them until I had the ultrasound done. That day, I showed my mom the picture of the ultrasound. I was having a girl. I always wanted a little me. I was excited! Even though I had proof that I was in fact pregnant, people had a hard time believing me because my stomach had been extremely flat.

With my parents finally knowing that I was pregnant, and finally living in our own home, I was sure things would turn out for the better. Unfortunately, they didn't. Greg kept drinking. There had been many many nights he had gotten violent. When he wasn't being violent, he would cry a lot about his brother. He would say that he wanted to die too. He always stated that the people in his head told him to kill himself.

During Greg's meltdowns and ordeals, I cried as I held my stomach. I didn't know how to deal with this. I had never been around somebody who was an alcoholic and was suicidal. I had never been around someone as toxic as he was. At the time, I was hopeless, because I didn't see a way out. I was pregnant. What was I going to do?

His entire family began to hate me. They accused me of not being nice to him. They claimed that I was leading him to drink. Sadly, there were times that I actually believed it! I questioned if I was too outspoken. Was it my fault because I didn't baby him? But when I used to baby him, things didn't get any better. When I used to try to reason with him to only have one drink, I couldn't get through to him. All he wanted to do was sit there and drink while playing his video games. To justify what he did, he said that he had a right to do so.

I was left feeling alone, 18, and pregnant. I had no idea what I was trying to do. I didn't understand how to keep my little family together. During that time, I had to admit to myself that I wanted to grow up too fast. I wasn't prepared for any of this.

I became really fed up with Greg. I was tired of all of his drinking. I was sick of him crying, throwing himself down the stairs, hitting his head on the wall. There had been many times I sat there screaming, "what are you doing? STOP." I constantly told him that he needed help!

Instead of seeing that I was trying to help him, Greg would just throw it back in my face. He accused me of not loving him. He stated that nobody loved him. Followed by, "I'm going to kill myself." After making these remarks, he would just lay on the ground and cry as he yelled for his brother. . . screaming his name. All while he would punch himself in his head.

After a while, his sister-in-law started to notice that there had been times he did do things for attention. I was a little relieved. Finally, someone besides me had noticed. A lot of times I felt like he was faking everything. He would drink one beer and walk around like he was drunk. I started to keep track of how much he drank.

I was certain that he was attention seeking because it was impossible for one can of beer to get him drunk. His tolerance for drinking had already been high because he drank so much. When

I would say anything to him about his drinking, he told me that he was a man. Men who worked deserved to come home and have a drink. He insisted that it was always just one, so there was no harm in him having it.

What Greg didn't understand was that the issue wasn't him having a beer. The real issue behind everything that happened was that Greg could never handle the truth very well. So any time he was told the truth, he resorted to drinking and attention seeking instead of facing it!

The more I watched him performing, I started getting very fed up. I was very annoyed with him. He wasn't acting out because he needed help. He did it because he just wanted attention.

I stopped feeding into his drama, so Greg's behavior became more extreme. One day, I was driving back to our house from a family event. During the car ride, Greg sat moping. Out of nowhere, he opened the car door and rolled out of the car. I started screaming and started to panic. I stopped the car as quick as I could, and started running in the direction he had rolled.

Once I reached Greg, I grabbed him. I screamed as I cried. I could not believe that I had just watched his entire body sliding down the road from my rearview mirror. His entire leg and arm were scraped up. At this point, I was certain that he was literally losing his mind.

Instead of calling the authorities for help, I called his family. This is what I did anytime he threatened to kill himself. It had become a habit. I never wanted to call the police on him for wanting to kill himself. Mainly because I never wanted him to get arrested. I couldn't allow that to happen because I couldn't live without him. He was the father of my unborn child.

Unfortunately, things didn't go as I'd hoped. I tried to explain what happened to them in as much detail as possible. I really thought that they would see that he needed help. But they didn't. Once again, he was babied by them and I received backlash from them.

This cycle repeated itself so much that we stopped getting along with Greg's family. That left me all alone to deal with him during his episodes. I was lost. I was nowhere near equipped enough to deal with his mental illness. At the time, I just thought he was a drunk being a drunk.

In hindsight, I wish I would have pushed him to seek help. All of the clues were there. It was more than attention seeking behavior. I recall one episode that pointed to there being a serious problem. On that particular night, I was in the kitchen cooking. He came in and started to argue with me. Suddenly, he told me to stab him. I couldn't believe this was really happening. I refused. He grabbed my hands and tried to make me cut him. I tried pulling back because I didn't want to stab him.

What horrified me the most was the look in Greg's eyes as he grabbed my hand over and over again. He looked crazy as he stared me straight in the eyes telling me he wanted me to kill him. It was as if he was not all there. Finally, I was able to let go of the knife one last time. Thankfully, he left me alone.

That night, I sat crying my eyes out. He had been so much stronger than me. I couldn't believe that he tried to make me stab him in the stomach. I knew from the look in his eyes he was serious too. He really meant what he said, he wanted to die, and he was trying to have me kill him!

I started to feel like he was trying to get his wish and frame me for it. I felt like I was between a rock and a hard place. Where was I going to go? What was I going to do? Before all of this, I thought we were going to be a happy family. But out of the blue, everything turned into a complete mess. And it was all because I trusted my own emotions.

CHAPTER 10: **OH BABY!**

Although I was going through hell and back with Greg, I still had someone to calm me down. My baby girl. Being pregnant with her brought me so much peace and joy. After the morning sickness went away, I was in complete love with my pregnancy.

I finally was able to enjoy food again, which meant that I could finally eat again. Because I was finally eating, and not starving from being so sick, I ate any and everything I wanted. For the first time in my life, I weighed more than 115lbs because I had blown up from eating so much. I would wake Greg up in the middle of the night crying because I wanted a box of Twinkies. He would reluctantly get up and go buy them, just so that I would stop crying. And I sat and ate the entire box to end my cravings.

To my surprise, my mom threw me a baby shower. It was a very simple shower with her church friends. Even though I was having a child out of wedlock, they gifted me with everything that I needed. We were very blessed to say the least.

Immediately after the baby shower, I took everything back to my house. I was excited. I enjoyed the process of setting up all the baby's things in my big walk-in closet. It was pure bliss to see all of the pink and purple everywhere. As I waited for my baby girl's arrival, I sat every day looking at all of her stuff.

My brother's girlfriend was pregnant at the same time as well. Just as everyone made sure my baby had everything, they did the same for them. As we waited for our babies, we waited without stress or worry about the necessities.

My baby girl came two weeks late. Even though she was late, she was the perfect little teeny thing. She weighed 5lbs and 6oz and had a head full of hair. I cried as they laid her body on mine. I was her mommy. I loved her at first sight. She was the best thing that ever happened to me. She brought me so much joy.

I was now a 19-year-old mom with an alcoholic boyfriend. Greg continued to focus on playing video games and drinking, even after the birth of our daughter. By then, I didn't even care about him anymore. I was only concerned about my daughter. All I wanted to do was sit in the rocking chair all day and hold my baby.

When she wouldn't latch on to my breast during feeding, I became worried. Even then, Greg did not help. Scared and hopeless, I called the one person who I knew would be able to help, I called my adoptive mom crying. I did not know what was wrong with me. I did not know what to do. After hearing what was wrong, she told me to come over.

Once home, I laid in her bed and she helped my little baby to latch on. She even taught me different positions to hold her in while feeding her. I was both relieved and grateful to my mom for sharing her wisdom with me.

After my daughter started to feed regularly, I decided to go back home with her father. Looking back now, I can admit that this was probably one of the stupidest things that I have ever done. He did not help me with her. I really felt like a single parent. To make matters worse, it even seemed like he became jealous of her and I's relationship. I could tell that he felt left out. He even voiced his concern.

I truly didn't care at the time. I honestly didn't know that it was important to balance the two relationships. I didn't see that I was in the wrong for truly not caring about him anymore. Instead of empathizing with him, I kept telling him, "this little baby needs me."

I did everything I could to be the best mother that I could be to my daughter. I took pride in caring for her. So when her skin began to break out, I blamed myself. I felt like I was failing as a mother, because no matter what I put on her skin, it remained dry, crusty, and flaky. This continued until we finally took her to the doctor. I was told she was lactose intolerant, and had severe eczema. It became imperative to change her formula.

I was crushed. I never wanted to put her on formula. I only wanted to breastfeed her. But because I honestly wasn't willing to change the way that I ate, I had to. Her breakouts were terrible. I was almost embarrassed to take her out in public because her cheeks were oozing all the time. She could not stop scratching. My poor baby was very uncomfortable, and cried a lot because of it. Whenever we would get one thing under control, new allergies would surface. Because of this, she was either always on Benadryl or Zyrtec and had cream everywhere.

It was very difficult being a young mother and dealing with this. Especially with her father being there but not really. I hated feeling helpless. I was so mad; all I wanted was some help from her father. I wished he would get off of his stupid game. I just wanted to be able to take a shower without feeling like a bad mom because my baby was crying in her crib.

One day, I became fed up. I kept calling Greg, but he didn't answer. I calmly sat the baby down, went into the garage, and got a hammer. I then smashed his game into several pieces all over the garage floor.

While I smashed the game, I screamed at him like a psychopath. I was over him acting like a freaking child! I know smashing his game was probably not the best way I could have handled that situation. But everything inside of me was fed up. I had grown tired of him. It started to be too much for me to bear. Because we were so young, we had no clue how to be a family. I didn't even understand who I was as a woman. Let alone how to please somebody who was never meant for me. We were living in complete chaos.

Breaking his game was pointless. He called his mother. She bought him a brand-new handheld game. I couldn't believe it. The only good thing that came out of that situation was that he did kinda watch our daughter. While playing his game, he would lay her in his lap and play. This bothered me because he still wasn't giving her any attention. When I was with her, all I wanted to do was hold and talk to her. I couldn't understand how he was more involved in a game than he was with his own daughter.

I honestly thought that Greg would change once our daughter was born. I assumed that his mood swings would stop, but they never did. I naively thought that he would feel that he now had more of a reason to live. I quickly realized that I had been trying to live in a fantasy world

With this realization, and maybe a little disgust, I became cold and heartless towards him. Whenever he said he wanted to kill himself, I started telling him to do it. What's ironic is that the first time that I told him to do it, he looked at me like I was the crazy one. I told him he kept saying it for attention. I literally started to antagonize him. Greg's only response was, "see, I told you you didn't love me."

By this point, I just didn't care anymore. No matter what I said or what I did, everything was always going to be my fault anyway. I was over his drinking. I was over him threatening to kill himself. So every time he started to threaten to kill himself, I went to the kitchen, grabbed the knife, handed it to him, and would walk away.

I became callous because I didn't know how to keep handling this situation. He constantly lied about it to others. They believed him, even though they didn't know the half of what I was dealing with behind closed doors. We literally fought over everything and nothing at all. He disgusted me. Everything he did upset me, including the way he ate his food.

Eventually, I started being that woman who complained about everything. He now started to be a child in my eyes. A big grown baby. Someone I never envisioned as a husband-to-be. The last straw for me was an argument we had. We were in the bedroom upstairs. I was holding our daughter as we argued. He lost his mind again. He grabbed her bassinet, the one which I usually sat her down in when upstairs, and threw it across the room. My first thought was, "you could have killed my baby had I placed her in there."

I knew then there was absolutely no way I could be with this man anymore. My daughter could have died. He knew I was about to set her down in the crib and he threw it at the wall. I just kept imagining my life without my daughter. I knew I couldn't keep putting her through this. I packed some of my daughter and my belongings, and went to my friend's house who lived down the street from us.

Before we left, he fell on the floor crying. He said he was so sorry. He couldn't believe that I was leaving him. No matter what he had to say, my mind was already made up. Everything I endured, even during my pregnancy, was horrible. Now that she was 4 months old, and these things continued to go on, I couldn't take it anymore.

I could no longer take his unprovoked outbursts. I could no longer live with the suicidal threats. What's even worse was that I didn't even like the person I had become. I now refused to keep feeling like him going crazy was my fault.

Although I did not know how to prevent what had occurred, I knew I had to keep my baby safe, no matter what. I was no longer stupid and naïve—I was fed up!

2 Corinthians 6:14 -"be not unequally yoked with unbelievers: for what partnership has righteousness with lawlessness or what fellowship has light with darkness."

CHAPTER 11:
FROM BAD TO WORSE

When I went to my friend's house, I knew it wasn't going to be an option for very long. At the time that I left my home, I didn't know what options were available to me. I didn't have time to think about it either. All I knew in that moment was that I had to get out of there! That night, Greg was angry that I left. But I honestly didn't care anymore, and I didn't plan on going back to him.

After leaving him, I took things one day at a time. During that time, Greg bought everything that our daughter needed. So she was fine. Things seemed to be going well for us. For the first time in a long time, I started to live again.

While at my friend's house, I started to drink. I was a lightweight. I hadn't drank in a long time because of being pregnant and breastfeeding. So we started drinking a little every day to ease me back into it. I was really enjoying myself.

I had already moved on from Greg. I started having sex with my friend's brother's friend. I was trying to fill the void of being alone. I had been with Greg for a long time. Even though I felt alone while being with him, it was nothing compared to how I was now feeling.

Before, I was with my daughter all day. But now that I was separated from Greg, he would pick her up to spend time with her. This meant that I was kid free. I didn't know what to do with myself, or my time. So when the next-door neighbors announced that they were going to drink that night, I decided that I wanted to go there too.

When I told my friend of my plans, she immediately didn't want me to go. I don't know if it's because her brother was going to be there as well. But I told her that I was perfectly fine. Besides, I'd known both of them for years, I wasn't worried. I knew that I would be safe.

That night I was excited when I arrived at the neighbor's house. Music was playing; different colored lights were on, and we were having a good time. Aside from me, there were three guys there that night. A white guy, an Asian, and somebody from the islands.

As we sat enjoying each other's company, we drank. But I didn't have very much to drink. Even though this was the case, everything around me started spinning. I quickly became sick. I had never felt like this before. Despite how I felt, I kept partying. I assumed what I was feeling would go away. I kept dancing around to the music.

Suddenly the three guys started touching me at the same time. My boobs, which were still huge from breastfeeding, popped out of my shirt. This excited them. The next thing I knew was that one of them took my pants off. I felt all of their hands all over my body. My head was pounding by now and kept dropping. The room was now spinning. I could see them sitting around, each touching themselves as they peered over my body.

One of them picked me up and sat me right on his penis. This was done right in front of the others. I was then passed between the three of them. They bounced me up and down. I remember throwing up in my own mouth and swallowing it. I heard laughter and them talking about what they were doing to me. I don't know how long this lasted. Somehow, I started crawling up the stairs. They smacked my butt extremely hard. I could feel stinging all over my body. They continued to have their way with me all the way up the stairs as they laughed. My knees were bruised. My body was in an immense amount of pain. My head was still spinning.

I finally made it to a room. Once inside, I laid down on a workout machine. My eyes were rolling in the back of my head. I could hear them laughing and talking as I went in and out of consciousness. I could feel them pulling up my body so they could take turns. At one point, my head hit the workout machine hard. I grabbed it and started crying. That hit kinda woke me up.

I went and laid down in a bed in a different room. The white guy came in and started having sex with me again, condomless. I felt my eyes closing; I laid there as he said he loved me. I came-to because of the pain I felt in my body. It hurt so bad. I immediately felt sick. I tried to get out of the bed. I remember I wanted to shower. A feeling of disgust blanketed my body. I needed to wash it off. I just wanted to shower. I had to wipe away the dirtiness.

I remember laying in the bottom of the tub and waking up to cold water on me the next day. I couldn't believe how my body felt. I had bruises everywhere. My head hurt so bad. I ran next door as quickly as I could. My friend saw how upset I was. Immediately, she said she knew there was a reason why she didn't want me there alone. She went to the store and got me a feminine product to flush out my private area. When I inserted it, I screamed. The burning pain I felt was unreal. I cried.

Several questions bombarded my mind all at once. Why did I go? Was this rape? I wasn't sure. I didn't say no. I was flirting with them. Why did I put myself into this position? I was lost. I laid on the bathroom floor unsure of how to answer my own questions—as pain covered every inch of my body. I was sore from my head down to my feet. My body was already showing signs of bruising. You could literally see finger marks on different parts of my body. I was so sick, my head was spinning, and I continued to ask myself why I was there by myself!

I blamed myself instead of the three sexual predators who had taken advantage of me. I let it happen. I needed to go. I couldn't stay in that house! I couldn't bear to live next door to where I had been raped. I never called the police. What was I going to say ? I felt dumb! I didn't want to sit and have to explain myself to anybody.

I took it as a lesson learned. I decided I would never put myself in that type of position again. I would never let anybody else pour me anything to drink, I would always get my own. I don't know why the alcohol hit me differently that night. Still, to this day, I have never felt like that even on my drunkest nights. But I honestly can't sit here and say that I was drugged because I don't know what happened.

One of the reasons why I just allowed things to be was because one of the men's family was connected to the police. I felt like even if I did come forward, no one would believe me over him. I knew the circumstances surrounding the situation didn't look good at all. I didn't want to go through the process of being blamed for what had happened to me. I already felt shame and guilt. I felt like it had been my fault, and that I was stupid for getting used like a toy.

To help myself to cope with what transpired, I told myself it was just sex. I was fine. I started to act as if the gruesome things that happened never happened.

Unfortunately, I am reminded of its occurrence from time to time. Sometimes, I see the man who have connections to the police around town. When we see each other, we always lock eyes, but say nothing.

Prior to writing this book, I never talked about that night again. I was too embarrassed to admit that one of my friends whom I trusted had betrayed me. And this betrayal resulted in three guys, two of which I did not know, having their way with me.

CHAPTER 12:
RESCUED BY MY SECOND FAMILY

When I decided to leave my friend's house after I had been assaulted, I didn't just go anywhere, like I had previously done. I actually thought about it. I picked up the phone and called a family friend, who was like my second family. Without hesitation, or a million and one questions, my "uncle" came to my rescue.

Once we arrived at their home, he said, "welcome home." In that moment, I felt so much safety and relief. It was exactly what I needed to hear after the torture I had just experienced.

I was excited to now be living with them. Their adoptive daughter, who was three years younger than me, was one of my best friends. She was my first black friend. We became so close growing up that we called each other cousins. I was no stranger to their home because it's the place I frequented for a very long time. Their home was the place I went to be tutored for math.

It was a safe place. It had always been a place of comfort for me. A place where I had no reservations about living with my daughter. There we had our own bedroom. It was perfect.

As perfect as things were, living with them was still an adjustment for me, as well as for my cousins. They were all still in school, and not used to me being there. They were also not used to seeing me weigh as much as I weighed. Neither was I.

When I had gotten pregnant with my daughter, I had gained a lot of weight. Although she was already 4 months old, I was still carrying a lot of the weight. I literally went from 115lbs to 198lbs. I was extremely insecure about it, and my cousin didn't make it any better for me. She used to say things that would drag me down, but was funny at the same time. She did it in a way that motivated me to do something about it.

She pressured me to workout with her. Although I was self-conscious, I went along. Together we would run around the block, do jumping jacks, sit-ups, and push-ups. She pushed me hard! As a result of our consistency, and her motivation, I lost weight really really quickly. I got back to being skinny. I felt like I could breathe again because I started to feel like myself again.

I was trying to rebuild and live a normal life again. So I went back to work at the fast food restaurant. Because it was right down the street from where we lived, I was able to walk there. While I worked, my mother babysat my daughter for me. Things were starting to fall into their proper place.

As a part of my rebuilding process, I decided this was a good time for me to get in touch with my biological grandparents. Yes, the ones who gave me up for adoption. Initially, we had small conversations on and off. With each conversation, they would ask if I wanted to visit them. Of course I wanted to visit them!

Shortly after our reconnection, I gave in. My daughter and I boarded a plane to Texas. I was excited. I didn't know what to expect. All I knew was that I was going to see my biological family. Once we arrived at the airport, we were picked up by a taxi. We were taken to my grandparent's home which was not too far from the airport.

The taxi stopped right in the front of this big house. My grandpa was right there waiting for us. This sight warmed my heart. My daughter instantly reached out to him. My grandpa treated her like a little princess the whole time we were there. I instantly felt as though we were finally home.

It was wonderful sitting listening to my grandpa. He had a thick accent which made everything he said sound hilarious. He was always talking mess. I laughed so much during this visit.

My step-grandmother looked exactly the same as I remembered her looking. Her hair was still super long. She still wore big old glasses. Seeing her brought back so many memories. Being with them again felt good, but made me sad at the same time.

One day, my grandmother and I were sitting in their upstairs living room (yes, their house was so big that it had an upstairs living room). She began to talk about the adoption. She told me that they tried to call us. That they had sent letters, but everything was being sent back or blocked. She reiterated that they never wanted to not be in our lives. They wanted to just be grandparents. They thought us having a younger family with siblings would be better for us.

I couldn't believe what I was being told. I couldn't wrap my head around everything. This means that my adoptive mom was the one who had stopped the communication, causing me to feel rejected by them. She allowed me to believe that they just didn't want us. She never once told me the truth. After this, I felt angry. But I didn't allow it to show.

I watched how they were with my daughter. How my grandpa would jump up so quickly every time my little baby would stand at the stairs and scream for him. I listened to how he called her princess and gave her whatever she wanted. I admired how she knew she had him wrapped around her finger. How they even took her shopping for more clothes.

Seeing how they treated her brought back memories. Watching him hold her reminded me of him treating me the same way. With so much love and compassion. It was amazing!

My amazement quickly vanished with one comment. As my grandpa sat in his chair he said, with his thick accent, "you're going to be just like your mother." I sat in disbelief! My heart was instantly broken. I knew that he had been estranged from her for many years, so this was the last thing that I wanted to hear.

He had nothing good to say about her. The only thing I knew about her was that she was on drugs, and she didn't take care of her children. Why would he say that I would be like her? What had I done to make him say that to me? I didn't know then, and I still don't know now.

Leaving my grandparents was bittersweet. I enjoyed most of the time I spent with them, with the exception of the conversation with my grandmother, and then the comment that my grandpa had made.

When I arrived home, my anger towards my mother grew. It was so bad that I avoided her for a while. Finally, I couldn't take it anymore. What my grandmother had told me was eating away at me. I needed to hear the other side of the story. So I went to my parents' house. I came straight-out and I asked my mother why she had done what was claimed. She looked shocked at first, but then she said that she thought it would be better for us. I was appalled!

My mother then started to make claims of her own to support her actions. She alleged my grandparents would call on my birthday, but not on my brother's. That they would send gifts in the mail on time for me, but not for my brother. I was shocked!

My grandparents and my mother told me different and conflicting things. I didn't know who or what to truly believe. I felt like there were a lot of secrets that needed to be revealed.

I wanted to know the truth once and for all. Who was I? Where did I come from? Why was I forgotten about? Why was I passed around and dumped somewhere? Why wasn't I ever checked on. Everything that I heard hurt me to the core. Why did I have to have these memories? Why couldn't I be back with my other siblings and just not know anything?

It's been 12 years since I went to Texas to visit my biological grandparents. I still don't fully understand, or know the truth. What helped me to move forward without knowing was understanding that God's plan for me has prevailed. I cannot feel like the child who was forgotten. Even if they didn't love me, He loved me. I had to stop holding on to the past and the things that made me feel more broken.

My wholeness came from me refusing to believe that I needed any of them to justify who I was. God knew all along. He had plans for me. I had to stop seeing myself as an unloved child, and stop allowing what I couldn't control, or change, to hold me captive. With that, I couldn't continue to speak negative things because I had become too wrapped up in my emotions and the pain from my past. I had to reject the lie that that was the only thing for my life.

I don't hate them. I'm not mad at them for not taking care of me. I didn't even need an apology from them to get to this place. I was able to forgive them without hearing their words. This was only possible because, at the time when everything had come out, I was seeing a counselor who kept telling me that I had to forgive. At first, I argued with her. I told her I didn't know how to. I kept explaining how mad I was at them for hurting me.

In the process of releasing those things, I realized something: by refusing to forgive them, I was only hurting myself. Because as long as I refused to let go, I was holding on to the pain. In that moment, I understood what is meant when they say, "let go, and let God."

Matthew 18 21:22- "Then came Peter to Him, and said, Lord, how oft shall my brother sin against me, and I forgive him? till seven times? Jesus said unto him, I say not unto thee until seven times, but until seventy times seven."

CHAPTER 13: **CYCLES**

My daughter's dad didn't come around often. When he did, I would yell at him and call him a bastard. I started to become a hateful and bitter person. He even acknowledged it. He would sit there and tell me that I changed, and he didn't understand why. I did change. I was tired of being lied on and mistreated. I decided I was now going to treat people how they treated me. I knew that it was wrong, but I was tired of experiencing hurt. I was tired of being a good woman and good mother and getting walked all over.

To protect myself, I started to build a really high wall around my broken heart. Being mean was now a defense mechanism. I'd be damned if I got hurt again. I started to take everybody with a grain of salt.

Even though I was extremely mean and nasty towards Greg, he would still bring diapers and things for our daughter. When he couldn't, or wouldn't, my aunt and uncle would help me out. You would have thought that that was enough, but it wasn't. For whatever reason, I started to steal everything.

I would walk into the store with my baby and an empty diaper bag. When no one was looking, I would shove things inside. I would put formula and food inside. I placed unpurchased shoes on her feet, wrapped a blanket around her, and walked out. Stealing became so easy for me that it almost became a sport.

With the passage of time, I got other people involved in it too. Together, we would grab a bunch of stuff and leave the store like nothing happened. Sometimes, we would do this a couple of times a day. The items we would steal ranged from jewelry, to clothes, to food. We literally stole until we became bored with the selection the store had left.

Stealing quickly became an addiction. So we pushed the limits. We started stealing from big department stores. The only thing that stopped me dead in my tracks was when one of my friends went without me and got caught. Even though I wasn't there with her, they told her that they knew about me. They said they were waiting for me to do it again, so that they could catch me too. After hearing this, I decided to never steal again. I was always too scared.

Now that I wasn't getting the adrenaline rush from stealing, I needed something else to cause me to feel like I was living on the edge. I found the perfect antidote. While visiting the town's Farmers Market one summer day, I met a light-skinned gangster who thought he was all that. As soon as we locked eyes, we started talking and flirting with each other. Because the conversation had been so good, I decided to take his number when he gave it to me.

Things moved pretty quickly between the two of us. I started sneaking him in and out of my aunt's house through the window. I did this because I knew that nobody would approve of him. He was a little older than I was. He wore his pants really low and always smelled like weed. I knew there was no way I could introduce him to anyone.

I should have known that I had no business trying to be with him. Instead of using my head, I let my emotions and my flesh control everything when it came to him. I couldn't understand why I was even attracted to him. Unlike me, he never held a job for very long. All he did was live off of women, smoke weed, and hang out at the corner store all day.

To justify his actions and lifestyle, he kept talking to me about the black man's struggle. How hard it was for him to get a job out here in a white town. He said that they always looked at his appearance, how he was tatted up and wore red, and judged him. I fell for every excuse he made.

I wasn't used to a man like him. There had been something that intrigued me. It made me feel like I was living on the edge. I would walk down to the park a couple of days a week and watch him play basketball. I knew that I was lowering my standards as I sat on the park bench. After a while, I started to be like him . . . not doing anything with my life.

Out of the blue one day, I got a phone call from his baby's mother asking me who I was. I was shocked! I knew nothing about her until she called. When I questioned him about her, he said that they weren't together, but they lived in the same house. He said he slept in the other bedroom. I was furious. So I went to her house. Instantly, we started yelling at each other. Looking back now, I don't even know why I thought I could go to somebody else's house and talk to them crazy. But I did.

With the walls, and my new mentality, I became a little bit bolder and more outspoken than I had ever been in my life. When she called, we yelled and called each other names—nothing was solved or changed. He continued to live with her, and still snuck in and out of my window. At that time, I didn't care because I was so stupid and head over heels about him.

When he complained about them not having any food for his son, I would take my hard-earned money and go buy a bunch of baby food. Instead of handing it to him, I would go to their house and set it on their doorstep and leave. I was really focused on trying to be the best girlfriend that I could be to him. I was hoping that he would see that I actually cared about his child.

During this time, I started saving money to get my own apartment. I was finally able to spread my wings for the first time since moving in with my aunt and uncle. My uncle found out that I had a guy in my bedroom and became pretty angry. Afterwards, I knew that it was time for me to move out as soon as possible.

I was ecstatic when I found a two-bedroom townhouse. It was my first place that I had gotten by myself. I could afford to pay the rent with the government assistance I was getting. It was located up the road from my job, which meant that I could walk back and forth to work, and drop my daughter off at the daycare across the street from us. I felt like my life was finally working itself out.

Unfortunately, once I moved into my new place, things didn't work out as I had planned. Instead of it just being my daughter and I living there, he came too. He now decided to not just come and go, but live there. I had a grown man in my house who didn't contribute financially.

All he did was drain me financially. When he first came around me, I didn't smoke weed. Instead, I would drink the cheap stuff: vodka and Boone's Farm. He, on the other hand, was a chronic weed smoker, who always tried to pressure me into smoking with him. I would say no. But he kept insisting. He said that I was always stressing, and it would calm me down. So I gave in. At first, it made me paranoid, but then I became used to it.

I would sit and smoke with him all day. This caused him to build up enough courage to ask me for money to buy weed. At first, it was $20 here and there. But it soon grew to $80 and then $150.00. He had perfect timing with his requests. He always managed to wait until I got paid to come with his hand out. He would always say that he would take what he bought and "flip" it. This never happened because he ended up smoking it all.

I was spending a lot of money on weed and whatever he wanted. He waited until payday to request whatever he wanted from me. I always gave into him because he was extremely nice to me around that time. I truly cared about him and wanted to be the "ride or die" loyal girlfriend.

I allowed a lot of things to slide by during that time. He smoked as much weed in the house as he wanted with his friends. While I was working all day, they remained there hanging out. His free-loading friends literally lived on my couch part-time. My home quickly became the hangout spot.

One day, one of them brought ecstasy into my house. I became really angry because weed was one thing, but I wasn't going to allow all these other drugs in my house around my child. I started to question myself, whose house did they think this was? My intent had never been to work to support a grown man and his habits. I was once again in a toxic cycle that I did not know how to get out of.

He started to talk crazy to me. Now we were constantly fighting. I had never been with someone who was so comfortable with cussing me out and calling me all types of names. To justify what he was saying, he would follow it up with, "you're just acting like one." It became so bad and frequent that he started yelling and arguing with me before I had to go to work.

Things continued to escalate between the two of us. One day, as we were arguing, he reached over and punched me in the back of my head in front of my daughter. She started screaming at the top of her lungs. She was terrified. I was in shock. I didn't know how to react, or what to do in that moment. I still had to go to work, so I didn't have a choice but to pack her and her things into her stroller, and take her to daycare on my way there.

Leaving her at daycare was probably one of the hardest things I've had to do. She kept crying; I knew she was scared and worried. I was stressed out. I couldn't even work a full day that day. So I left early and picked up my daughter before walking back home.

Before this point, I never let anything affect my job. But after that, I started getting in trouble at work because he would come and hang out in the lobby. He did this a bunch of times throughout the day. He was trying to get me fired. When that didn't work like he wanted it to, he had his father call my job and threaten them.

Although I had nothing to do with their actions, I got suspended for two weeks. I cried so much. I didn't know how I was going to pay my bills. When I got back to my house after being suspended, everybody was there drinking and partying in the middle of the day. I was furious. I kicked everybody out. I grabbed his CD case and I threw it out the door. At this point, I was angry. He shoved me into a pile of bushes and started screaming at me. He raised his fist up to me as he threatened to hit me again. He did this while his friend watched. I couldn't believe what was going on.

Thankfully, that relationship didn't last very long. He decided to move to California to be closer to his baby mother and his son. I was both happy and relieved. He didn't allow me to live in complete peace though. He would call my house phone and threaten me.

After he left, and when I returned to work, I put all my attention and focus into working to rebuild my reputation, and on getting more hours again. Although they did not fire me, they decreased the hours that they would allow me to work.

Shortly after returning to work, I was invited to a Quinceanera. Initially, I wasn't sure about going. Honestly, I felt a little bit out of place. But I decided to go anyway. It gave me a reason to dress up and finally get out. Besides, everybody at work was going, and the place where it was being held wasn't too far from my house. That meant that I could easily walk over there and back.

Once I arrived at the Quinceanera, my excitement ceased. I started to feel a little bit out of place, so I stood in the corner by myself. While there, I noticed this super cute Hispanic man staring at me. I watched him as he danced and knew instantly that he was a showoff. He was definitely trying to get my attention. Instead of giving in to him, I acted like I didn't see him. He had been one of several men that night trying to get my attention.

Although I could feel his gaze, and caught him staring at me several times, I walked past him like it was no big deal. I knew I was taunting him. Little did he know, I was taunting myself. While walking past him the smell of his cologne seduced my nostrils. I remember thinking he smelled amazing.

I assume he couldn't take my disinterest in him any longer, so finally he, Josh, asked me to dance. I gave in and said yes. I couldn't resist him any longer when he looked like a version of Antonio Banderas. I was happy I gave in because we danced all night. He even sang in my ear. I was in love, despite the fact that he kept apologizing for his English.

I really enjoyed his company that night. We danced. We both laughed hysterically when he told me that I was going to be his wife. I was like, "yeah, right," but he kept saying he was very serious. After a while, the look in his eyes gave me the feeling that he meant what he said, as crazy as it sounded.

Prior to leaving that night, we continued to have small talk. He asked things like: where did I work, which I told him. He inquired about where I lived, I told him sort of, but wouldn't disclose where. No matter how good he danced, or how much he had promised to marry me, the fact still remained that he was a complete stranger.

At the end of the night, we went our separate ways. A couple of days later my coworkers started telling me that a man kept calling asking for me. Not only that, but he would come in looking for me, but was unable to catch me working. I was shocked. I could not believe it!

I was forced to believe it when he showed up as I was working one night. As soon as he told me that he had been looking for me, we both smiled. He admitted that he had driven to Jack in the Box every day since I told him that I lived close to there. I was flattered. I still couldn't believe that he had actually been searching for me. No one had ever been this persistent in my life. I was impressed.

As we stood staring at each other, I couldn't help but admire him. He was about six feet tall. He had a little bit of salt and pepper hair. He was handsome to say the least.

He ended up waiting around for me until it was my lunch break. This not only gave me butterflies, but it made me blush. On my break, we talked more. He told me that he lived and worked in

Reno, Nevada. But he wanted to come and visit me another day. I liked the sound of that.

Because I didn't have a cell phone, we would talk for hours on my house phone. Even though I had a hard time understanding what he was saying because of his thick accent, and didn't know exactly what to say, I enjoyed the calls. He was so nice. He was a man who always made me laugh. He joked all the time too. He was so refreshing and different from what I was used to.

I enjoyed him so much that I finally invited him over to my place for dinner. I was excited and nervous at the same time. I didn't have a lot of money, so I bought some frozen chow mein, and added stuff to it along with white rice and extra vegetables.

To my surprise, he was excited as well. We had decided that he would come late in the evening because he had to work his construction job late, and needed to shower before coming over. To eliminate the need for him to prolong coming to my place, I told him he could shower and get dressed for the evening here.

I remember being extremely excited and nervous about what I was going to wear. I was certain that I wouldn't be doing anything inappropriate with him because I had started my cycle. To put him on notice, and so that he wouldn't try anything, I left the entire big box of tampons on the top of the back of the toilet.

When he arrived at my house, my nostrils were filled with his scent, even though he was dirty. He smelled so good. He smiled so big. He joked around with me, even though it was evident that he was exhausted from working a long day.

After he showered, we ate. Although it wasn't a fancy meal, he made sure to express how appreciative he had been. He even complimented me on the way that I kept my house neat. He told me how much he liked my daughter and wanted to have kids one day.

We ended up talking for hours that night without realizing that so much time had passed us by. I decided to allow him to stay the night because of how late it was.

The next morning, at his request, he drove me around. He insisted because he didn't want me walking everywhere, or asking others for rides. I needed to go to several places to get the money I needed to pay my bills, so I took him up on the offer. He literally took me to church and several other places to hustle up money to get things paid. I wasn't embarrassed that he was witnessing all the transactions. He didn't say much during the entire process. He actually stayed quiet. When he did speak, he told me that he could have helped me. That he would have given me the money that I needed.

I was blown away. I had never had anybody tell me that before. Instead of taking him up on his offer, I told him that I was fine. I assured him that I was going to have the money I needed for the next month.

After that first night, and part of the next day together, we started spending more time with each other. He started driving back and forth from his job to my house. He took me and my daughter out to eat a lot as well. He was always checking in before he came over to make sure we didn't need anything. He would even help cook and clean. He was always so gentle with me. I wasn't used to it. But I quickly fell in love with it.

The euphoria that I had been experiencing was suddenly challenged when his phone started to ring repeatedly. He couldn't answer it because he had been showering. Instead of telling him, or ignoring it, I allowed my insecurities to guide me. I grabbed a hold of it and peered at the screen to see who was calling back to back. When I saw that there was a female's name on the caller ID, I decided to answer it without hesitation.

I told the woman on the other end of the phone in a nice but bragging tone that he was in my shower. In the same breath I informed her that we were together, to which she didn't say much.

As soon as he got out of the shower, I let him know that I answered his phone. He wasn't upset. He wasn't nervous. He straightforwardly told me that the woman on the other end was his girlfriend for the last five years. He assured me that they didn't live together because she was a cat lady amongst other reasons.

I was frustrated. I felt like he lied to me. I knew everything seemed too good to be true. As nice and attentive as he had been to me and my daughter, I would have never guessed that he had a girlfriend. Not to mention the amount of time he spent with me. I told Josh that I wasn't going to deal with this. He told me he felt sorry for her and that she wouldn't give him a child, or green card after all these years. Aside from hanging out with her from time to time, he had already decided he was done with her.

The conversation quickly turned. He asked if he could move in with me because he was spending so much time driving back and forth. Josh no longer saw the need to keep driving back and forth. At first, I was reluctant, but after going back and forth with him, and becoming even more frustrated, I gave in. I knew my life had been easier with him.

To make room for his belongings, Josh told my ex to come and get his things that he had left behind when he went to California. Initially, he wasn't happy about Josh. He continued to call and threaten the both of us all the time. Josh didn't pay him any mind. He told him that there was no need for any drama. Surprisingly, he finally came, got his stuff and left us alone.

As Josh went to pack up his belongings from the little room he had been renting, I made room in my house for a man that I really didn't know. I had been dating him for only a month at this time. He wanted me. So I was excited again because I felt like I had a family again. Especially because he instantly started paying all the bills in the house. This relieved me of a lot of stress.

Now, for the first time, I didn't want for anything. Things became too easy. Things seemed too perfect. What I didn't realize was that monsters come in all different shapes. I would come to wish that I would have never met the man from the dance. . .

CHAPTER 14:
MARRIED . . .TO THE DEVIL

I honestly couldn't have been any happier. I didn't have to stress about bills anymore. I didn't have to go without anything anymore. My life finally became easier, even in the face of my daughter's dad getting upset because I think he knew that this relationship was serious. My new relationship caused him to start seeing her more. He would pick her up on the weekends, which, honestly, I was okay with because Josh and I could go on date nights and get to know each other better.

Josh seemed so perfect for me. He always held my hand and took care of me. Josh used to always sing to me in Spanish. It was so beautiful. He always treated me like such a lady. I felt very spoiled. He was constantly telling me how beautiful I was while showing me off to all of his friends and all of his family. I never had that before, and they actually liked and respected me. They truly embraced me like family. It wasn't like the hate I experienced with Greg's family. Everything was a new fresh feeling.

I loved getting together with them and having family dinners. They taught me more Spanish. Despite the language barrier, they really were intentional with making us feel included. They loved my daughter. I thought to myself, "this is how family is supposed to be." Life was perfect, and my heart was finally happy!

Josh had no issue stepping into fatherhood. He threw my daughter's first birthday party without hesitation. He spared no expense making sure she had everything she needed and wanted. All the way down to making sure her bike, bed, and piñata, were all of her favorite character, Dora. Everything was planned out with so much thoughtfulness. I really didn't have to do anything, or ask him for anything. He just did things. This made me so grateful, and I appreciated him all the more.

At that time, I enjoyed everything about him. I became so comfortable with him. He was one of the first people I opened up to about my family. Even though he knew the truth about them, he was so very kind to all of my family, and never let his knowledge of the truth show.

As things progressed, our conversations progressed too. He started talking to me about babies. He asked me if I would give him a child. I told him I was scared because I didn't want to be a single mom again and struggle. Josh promised me he wouldn't do that to me.

I hated being alone with my daughter. I couldn't imagine having two kids and being alone. I never believed in forever with anyone because I didn't believe that's how it really worked. Even though this was the case, I told him yes, without realizing that I had made an agreement with the devil.

I overlooked the fact that Josh seemed so desperate and so serious. This was due in large part because he acted as if having a child was something he'd wanted his whole life. There was no way I could say no. We wasted no time. And neither did my ovaries. I got pregnant pretty quickly.

Soon after the pregnancy came the ring. One day, after Josh came home from work, my little baby girl walked up to me with a ring saying, "marry daddy Josh." Instead of being ecstatic and overjoyed, I was upset about how little the ring was. I had been under the impression that he definitely had more money and could afford something more than a small heart-shaped ring. Despite being upset, I said yes.

Immediately after the proposal came wedding planning. I didn't really want anything big because I was already pregnant, and the pregnancy was taking a huge toll on me. I was extremely tired all the time. So we decided to plan a very small wedding.

Now with the wedding plans solidified, it was time to shop for my wedding dress. Thankfully, it didn't take me very long to find my wedding dress. I was relieved because I wanted to hurry up and get married before my belly popped out even more. My relief quickly turned into panic when my mom decided to put my wedding dress on my sister. I don't know how exactly me showing her the dress turned into my sister trying on my dress. My mom grabbed the zipper and yanked it down causing it to break. I was so angry at her carelessness. Thankfully, she hurried up and found somebody to fix it. Things were back on track.

I was already a couple of months pregnant when our wedding day arrived. Although I could barely fit into my wedding dress because of my baby bump, I was content. I was finally getting my family that consisted of me, my husband, my daughter, and *our* new little baby in my belly. I finally would have the family that I always wanted. A-soon-to-be husband who loved and took care of me. A man who was working a good job. It made sense to be marrying this man that loved me so much.

We had our wedding at a little chapel. During the ceremony, I was upset because as I walked down the aisle, Josh's back was towards me. I couldn't understand why nobody told him to turn around to face me. I think everybody dreams about the day they can see their husband's face when walking down the aisle, and all I saw was his back. I didn't get to look in his eyes or see the look on his face. This was disappointing. But I let these feelings go after we said our vows. I was married. I was excited. I thought this was my forever. I wanted it to be my forever.

After the wedding ceremony, we went to a lake to barbecue some of the best meat that I had ever tasted in my life (or maybe it tasted so good because I was pregnant and hungry). Everybody kind of hung out. It wasn't anything big or fancy. But it was nice.

After the wedding, the first challenge that we encountered was with my daughter's dad. Someone who had only started to come around once my husband came into the picture, wanted joint custody. I was baffled. He didn't need to pursue anything in court because I was always reasonable with him, even when he wasn't reasonable with me. I never withheld our daughter from him. Even though I knew when he picked her up on the weekends that he got her that he would drop her off with family so that he could go out, I never said a word.

I never thought that I would see the day when someone who barely had my child, would try to take her away from me. I had my daughter all of the time. I just couldn't understand it. And I couldn't just allow him to take her without a fight.

I borrowed money from a family member and hired a lawyer. The day of court, he arrived without a lawyer. I thought I had the upper hand. We figured we had it in the bag. Greg was a suicidal alcoholic who hadn't been around consistently.

My confidence in the odds being on my side quickly vanished when our case was heard. Not only did Greg lie, but my lawyer was a joke. The person I had paid did absolutely nothing to represent me adequately. I couldn't believe that the judge had awarded him 50/50 custody of our daughter.

I was sick. I saw him laughing because he had gotten what he wanted by lying. I had to stomach his new girlfriend telling him "you won, you won." I was disgusted. Our child wasn't a prize. This wasn't a game. This was real life—my life!

I had never been away from my daughter for that long. The judge tried to ease things by granting phone calls during the time she was away from me for a week at a time. My heart broke. The image of my perfect family was no more.

As I prepared my child to leave me that first week, it was hard. I sat and cried as Josh held my daughter and I. He even wiped my streams of tears that flowed during the change of custody. I cried often for the first couple of months. I felt such a sense of emptiness because my daughter had been the only steady thing I had in my life. Through the ups and the downs my sweet baby had been there.

As I mourned, Greg enjoyed my pain. He often skipped to the door to get her while laughing. He didn't do this for anything else but to hurt me. He was nasty towards me too. Every time he would drop her off, he would call me a "nigger with an attitude." He would tell me that I should get hung. He would tell me to stop making her smell like a black person. He would say that she wasn't black, she was Puerto Rican.

As a result of Greg's behavior, we had someone come over and sit in our hallway on our stairs. While there, she would write down all the vile things that he would say during the change of custody of our daughter. We had an entire notebook full of the things he would say to us.

But things did not end there. Greg's girlfriend wasn't any better. My daughter came back home from visits with her ears pierced. Her ears became infected, but that didn't stop her from getting them re-pierced several more times. Once my daughter started to talk more, she told us that Greg's girlfriend was mean to her. She said the girlfriend called her a skinny dog and tried to feed her things that she was allergic to. Every time I told Greg about what she said, he just kept telling me I was crazy like the story in the Bible where the mother had the baby, and the woman who really wasn't the mother, was like, "okay, cut the baby in half." He claimed that what I was saying was just something to hold over his head.

Through everything I went through with Greg, my husband remained right there. He had my back the entire time. He helped me to keep things together while the situation was trying to drain the life out of me.

Thankfully, I was no longer working at the fast food restaurant. I was more of a stay-at-home mom who had a home daycare. Josh made sure that I had everything that I needed and wanted. Before marrying him, I walked everywhere. Now that I had married him, I went from walking to owning two cars. I literally felt like I had had nothing before I met him, as I constantly struggled working at a fast food restaurant. I felt like he was my saving grace.

My husband was here on a work visa that was going to expire soon. Even though he was still legal, I was afraid for him. There was no way I wanted him to go back to his country. I didn't know what I would do without him. The fear I felt was real. There had been many people in this area that were raided by ICE. Because their visas were no longer valid, they were sent back to their country. They had done nothing wrong either. They weren't causing trouble. They were illegal people who worked hard to get away from the poverty they lived in in their own country. They were just trying to provide for their families.

Because I knew what I had witnessed happen could just as easily be our reality, I didn't think twice when Josh asked me to help him get his papers. Why would I not help him when he's a great man who goes above and beyond for us? I felt like this was my opportunity to do the same for him.

We found a man who was an immigration lawyer. He told us the likelihood of him getting sent back was less than 5% because he came into this country legally, his visa was current, and we were about to have a baby. I was a little relieved. After starting the process, and paying somewhere around $8,000, we had to show pictures of our wedding documents. As well as proof that we lived together; that he was working, and had been paying taxes. As if that wasn't enough, he had to show proof that he had never been to jail.

Josh was extremely nervous. He verbalized how scared he was to go back. He expressed that he was the one that had financially supported his family from his wages here. How would he do that if he were unable to be here working? He and his brother started their business so that they could make their own money. He stated, although he hadn't seen his mother and all of his sisters in 10 years, he missed them, but wouldn't go back to even visit because of fear. He literally put supporting his family first. I admired him even more.

It hurt me that he was so scared of being deported. I saw the fear he expressed to me in his eyes. Even though we sometimes argued because I felt like he gave his family so much that we couldn't get what we wanted, I started to wonder who's going to take care of his family back home? Yes, there had been a time that I felt like they had been taking advantage of him and we argued about it. Which resulted in him making a phone call to them letting them know that he wouldn't be able to send as much because we were spreading ourselves thin. All of that didn't matter anymore. If he had gotten deported, who was going to take care of us? I was worried for us all.

Luckily, I wouldn't have to know the answers to these questions. Josh's papers finally arrived after what seemed like an eternity. That day he cried in my arms. He kept telling me, "thank you, thank you, I get to see my mom," with tears in his eyes. He literally hugged my legs while he stayed on his knees crying. The excitement and emotions I saw from my husband that day was something I had never seen before.

Unfortunately, it was something I would never see again. Shortly after receiving the papers granting him citizenship, I noticed the change in him. It bothered me to the point that we would argue about it. I asked him if that's all that he wanted from me the whole time, because that's what it seemed like to me. He knew he could never admit it because he had to be married to me for 6 years in order to keep his papers.

Prior to him receiving those papers, he was sweet as pie. He was gentle. Afterwards, he started to snap at me. He even wanted to sleep on the couch. I could not believe what was now unfolding. He started checking the mileage on the car. And accused me of crazy things.

Now that he had his papers, he kept telling me that I had nothing to do with him getting them. He stated that they were something that I was now holding over his head. He even went as far as saying that he wished he never allowed me to help him get them. I was completely dumbfounded!

Although we got over it, it was always in the back of my mind. His behavior was telling the true story. I started to think about something he previously said about his ex. That she wouldn't give him a child, or wouldn't help him get his papers. I started to feel like a dummy. I really thought he loved me and my daughter; that he wanted to marry me for me and not for his citizenship papers; that he really wanted the child that I was carrying because he wanted a child.

Despite the issues in our marriage, he was there when I went into labor with our son. I decided not to get an epidural because, after I had one with my daughter, I suffered from back issues. I was doing this drug free. Oh, the pain I felt was excruciating during the labor, but things were much better afterwards. My husband was holding one leg and his cousin, who was more like his sister, was holding my other leg. A couple of hours after sending myself through torment, hearing the doctors telling me to get an epidural, my baby boy, Daniel, was in my arms.

He was perfect. My little Danny. I was so excited when my daughter got home and finally held her little brother. She and my husband were both a huge help. To my surprise, Josh had no problem waking up or helping change Danny's diapers.

Although it seemed as though everything was perfect after the birth of Danny, it wasn't. It still never felt right having one of my children there with me all the time, and one going back and forth with her father. I don't feel like Josh ever truly understood what I was going through. He tried by being very accommodating. He was okay with planning stuff around the weekends that we had her. This made me feel a little better because I didn't want her to miss out on anything.

After giving birth to Danny and adjusting to now having two children, I spoke more to my biological mother. Even though we had reconnected a couple of years prior, we started to talk a lot more. During one of our conversations, she told me that she had found my biological father. I was beyond excited to hear this. I couldn't wait to call the man that I had never spoken to before.

When I called and spoke to him, my excitement quickly faded. I didn't feel the instant connection with him that I had felt with my mother. I was disappointed. I had hoped for something different to happen, but it didn't.

Thankfully, the disappointment I experienced with my father didn't stop me from continuing to connect further with my mother. To my surprise, Josh came home one day and asked me if I was ready to meet my family. I looked at him in shock, of course I was. This was a moment I had been waiting for.

We packed up the car and drove eight hours to Vegas to meet them. The moment that I had been waiting for my whole life was about to happen. As we drove, I sat there thinking, "what is she going to look like." I was always told my whole life that she was nothing but a crackhead. Honestly, that's how I expected her to look. So I braced myself as much as I could. My mother must have been just as excited as I was because she called me a couple of times during our drive. We had arranged to meet her at several places. But finally settled on meeting up at a gas station.

When we arrived in Vegas, it was really late at night. As we waited, I continued to brace myself for whatever I would see. All of a sudden, a broken-down suburban pulled up near us, and this woman jumped out. As her feet hit the pavement, I could hear her screaming, "Tachianna, hi, baby." To my surprise she was beautiful! This could not be the woman that everybody said was a crackhead. In that moment, I couldn't even cry—I had so many emotions going through my mind and my body at the same time. One emotion that stood out the most was a feeling of peace.

My mother embraced me for a quick second before jumping in the backseat with my children. They just stared at her. As she sat in the back with my babies, talking with my daughter and playing with Danny, I extended my hand backward and she held it. This was such a sweet first memory of being with my mom. As she held my hands, she kept telling me how beautiful I was. I was in heaven!

I guess the sight of what was transpiring was as beautiful as it felt to me because when I looked over at my husband, he was just smiling. I wished that we could stay in that moment forever, but we couldn't. My mother finally got out of our car and back into her truck. We then followed her to her house, or, should I say, what I believed to be her house.

As soon as we walked in, I realized that she lived in a squatter house with a bunch of other people. The house was big, with barely any furniture in the inside. As we walked through it to get to her bedroom upstairs, she told us to be quiet. Once inside, my eyes glanced at the bareness of the room. Aside from a mattress on the floor, there were a bunch of clothes in the closet.

Seeing my mother's living conditions didn't even bother me because she gave me so much attention. My mother hugged me like I've always wanted to be hugged. She told me I looked exactly like her and my biological father's mother. That night, we lay on the mattress together as she talked to me and told me a lot about her life. She shared with me how it wasn't easy. She told me something that I had always wanted to hear, that she wanted and loved us. I was moved to compassion hearing her express that she had never forgotten about us. I couldn't even be mad at her.

As she shared, I thought about the things she was sharing. She was such a broken woman who endured a lot in her life. It was crazy to even try to imagine what all she had gone through. She explained to me how I got removed from her. She didn't try to blame others. Instead, she owned up to her mess. She admitted that she was on drugs and was a prostitute during that time. She even told me something that no one ever uttered, that her mother sold her as a little girl for some drugs, and that she found her mother dead from a drug overdose. I was blown away.

As a little girl, my mother was found walking the streets of Oakland, CA. Everybody turned their backs on her after that. They didn't even address or acknowledge the traumatic things that she had gone through. She hadn't just decided to be a young drug addicted mother, who had gotten her children taken away, rather, she was trying to deal with the life she had been dealt. In that moment, I realized that she didn't know how to be a mom. She didn't know how to trust, or to love, because she wasn't loved.

When I heard her story, my heart wanted her with everything within me. As she talked we both sat crying like a bunch of crybabies. She kept apologizing to me over and over. But it wasn't needed. As far as I had been concerned, the past was the past.

My whole life I've grown up with other people who I didn't even look like. For the first time in my life, I was in the presence of someone that I not only looked like, but had the same mannerisms as me. And it didn't stop there. I had the same body type as her. We discovered that we said some of the same things. And had similar clothing too. For the first time in my life, I was with my mom, and nobody could take the feelings that I felt away from me.

The next morning, I had arranged to have breakfast with my biological father. We met in a parking lot. As soon as my mother saw him, she started to talk crap to him. She hadn't seen him since I was born. It was evident from their interactions that they both hated each other. It was so bad that they wouldn't take a picture together with me. I was so frustrated!

Being with my dad felt completely different than it was with my mom. Even though he gave me a soft hug as I sat in his car, we were almost silent. He was a lot quieter than my mother. I instantly became angry when I realized that his family was well-off compared to my mother. He had a support system.

I learned that I was a secret. He hid me from a lot of people. He had been married to his wife for a very long time; they raised his other five children together, but I was a hidden secret. He told me that some things were never meant to be known. That "thing" he was referring to was me. Hearing that hurt my heart to the core. I couldn't understand why I had to be a secret. Even though he told me that he loved me, I didn't feel or believe it.

During breakfast, I took my anger out on him. I told him about all of the bad things that had happened in my life. I pretty much blamed him for it. I was angry and it showed. I spoke to him with no respect. I was very emotional and did not want to be there with him. I was ready to go back with my mom. Even though I felt that way, we spent more time together. He took my daughter and I to the skating rink. It was very awkward. Nonetheless, I survived.

Once I arrived back to my mom's house, I met my younger brother. He was so cute. I could tell that he had been excited to meet me because he was so talkative. I also met a couple of my aunties, one of which I looked like. Although I enjoyed meeting them all, I sat around them quietly. It was different looking into the faces of people who you resemble after growing up sticking out like a sore thumb.

I wanted to stay in Vegas with my family, but knew I couldn't. The time had arrived for us to drive back home. I was so grateful to my husband for everything. I knew that this was going to be a new beginning for me; literally what I always wanted. I was on cloud nine. My dreams had come true. This made going home bittersweet for me. I knew that I had to visit again soon.

After our visit to Vegas, we were planning to take a trip to Mexico to see Josh's family. Before that trip, I found out that I was pregnant again. By this point, I was beyond exhausted. Josh had been working out of town a lot, and was only coming home on the weekends. I felt like a single mom again, but with money.

Nevertheless, I got my passport and planned to visit Josh's family. But instead of going as a complete family, I had decided to go while my daughter was with her father. I didn't want to argue with him about getting her passport.

Prior to the trip to Mexico, I found some woman's number. Before I decided on what to do, I called my friend for advice. I was both confused and frustrated. My friend told me to call the woman. Before I called her, I went through my husband's things as well. Prior to this point, I had never been this type of woman. I was appalled at what I found. Different love letters from women that we had been hanging around.

It was embarrassing to find out that my husband had brought me around women that he had been sleeping with. I was so clueless. One of his best friend's wives was one of them. All I could think was, "how dare he?" These women smiled in my face while they were sleeping with my husband. What made matters even worse was the fact that they too were married.

After I completed my little investigation, I called the number I had found. I wasn't even surprised to hear a woman's voice on the other end of the phone. I confronted my husband without delay. He told me that he was going to meet up with her at a hotel, but it never happened. He had the nerve to tell me that he was a man that had needs. I was livid to say the least. I couldn't believe him. He had the audacity to check the mileage on my vehicle and question me. When I was the faithful one in our marriage. I hadn't even thought of being with anyone else. But he was entertaining somebody else. I thought this was going to be the death of us.

While everything seemed as if it was now torn into tiny pieces, Josh left for work. He stayed gone for a week before he returned. During this time I cried. I knew that there was no way I was going to let my family fall apart. I packed up the kids and drove four hours to see him. We stayed in the nasty little hotel room he had been staying in and talked things out. In that moment, I refused to allow my family to fall apart. In hindsight, I wish that I had let it go. I didn't know that the worst was coming.

Although we reconciled, we continued to have issues. We literally argued during my entire pregnancy. We had a lot of trust issues. Even though this was the case, I wanted this baby more than anything. I had decided that I would have a midwife to assist me during the delivery. Although it wasn't legal in the area where I lived to give birth in a birthing tub, I was allowed to sit inside of it to help relax during labor. I took advantage of it.

When my baby was born, he came out blue. He didn't cry like his sister and brother had. I was scared. They told me to hold him, but I refused. I couldn't do it because I didn't know if he was alive or not. They continued to rub him repeatedly until he finally cried. In that moment, relief hit my body. Now, I would be able to connect with him.

My sweet baby was beautiful. Unlike my other children, his hair was gold—really, dark blond. His eyes were bluish-green. I thought he was just perfect. I was surprised when my husband questioned me about whether or not he was his son. I couldn't believe it. I had never been with anyone else. My mother had colored eyes. His brother had colored eyes. I told him each time he questioned the paternity of our youngest son that we could have a DNA test, which he declined.

We argued so much by that time that I was happy that he was gone. Yes, it was now very difficult having two young babies and a little toddler. I literally had three car seats and always had a stroller everywhere I went. But I loved my little family. They were perfect to me.

I focused all of my attention on my children. Everything became all about the babies. I no longer gave my husband any time. Besides, we constantly argued. I saw no need to give him any attention because he didn't appreciate it anyways. He became jealous of the children. I didn't even know what to say anymore. I couldn't understand why a man would get jealous over a child.

The wedge that was between my husband and I became bigger after the death of my brother. At that time, our youngest was about 2 months old. I saw my brother and his friends leaving Walmart. I offered to give them a ride home. They all piled into my car. I'll never forget how it was that day with sweaty boys with skateboards laughing, joking, and having a good old-time riding in my car on such a hot summer day. When my brother got out of the car, he said, "I love you sis, give me a hug." Instead of giving him a hug I said, "bro, I have to get home, I'm tired." He wouldn't let me off the hook that easy. He kept insisting that I gave him a hug. I laughed at him and said F-U. We laughed and I drove off.

When I got home, I unloaded the groceries and got the kids inside. Suddenly, my phone rang. It was my little sister. She was screaming her head off on the other end. It was that type of scream that you would never want to hear. I could hear sirens in the background as she kept screaming my little brother's name. I threw the babies in the car as fast as I could. I don't remember if they were buckled in correctly, or buckled in at all. Once I arrived at my mom's house, they said that there was an accident with my brother. He was being care flighted (airlifted to the hospital).

I was so confused. I was like, "what do you mean? he just got out of my car; he was fine 5 minutes ago. He was fine!" Apparently, my brother had been holding on to my play brother's car while riding his skateboard. My play brother had been going extremely slow. My little brother was never very coordinated, and was always awkward. His skateboard went over a small rock. This caused him to fall. When he fell, he hit his head and started to bleed. My older brother instantly started CPR on him. My mother said that when careflight came, they told her to say goodbye to him.

I remained at my adoptive mom's house trying to keep everyone calm. Despite what my mother had been told, it wasn't final. While there, I got a call from my mom. She said, "Tashi, he's gone." I started screaming and crying. I couldn't understand why him out of all of the kids. He was so innocent, so sweet, with an amazing spirit. He was always the first to help everyone. He always said that he was going to take care of people's horses. He was a black cowboy, who wore cowboy hats and loved playing guitar.

I replayed the last moments I saw him. Why didn't I just give him a hug! Why was F-U the last words that I said to him.

The community came together to support us. Everyone loved him. They donated everything that was needed. My parents didn't have to pay out of pocket expenses for the funeral. The church hosted a huge fundraiser car wash for him. The people from the community came and brought hundreds of dollars. They even brought food for a couple weeks.

My entire family came down too. My dad built him a beautiful coffin as a way to heal. He took a lot of pride in it too. I remember my mom and I crying after watching him outside building it.

His funeral was bigger than I had ever seen before. His horses led his body to rest. After the funeral, the community built a blue slide at the outdoor pool in memory of him. Every time I see kids sliding down it, it brings me so much joy.

After the funeral, I stayed at my family's house for a while. Going home, I felt empty. I couldn't function, and Josh was no support. He would tell me to get it together, that they needed me still, and that I couldn't grieve because I had kids to take care of. I heard him but didn't listen. I was dealing with postpartum depression, the loss of my brother, a husband who was working out of town, and my daughter's father who continued to verbally abuse me.

As I tried to balance everything while not breaking, it was time for us to take that trip to Mexico. My daughter stayed with her dad. The baby stayed with my adoptive mother because he didn't have a passport. Josh, Danny, and I got on the plane and headed to Mexico. We were excited when we finally got to Mexico City. The first person we saw was his sister. As soon as they saw each other, they embraced as they cried. I was exhausted by this time, but still had to hold things together because we had a couple of hours drive to get home.

This was my first time in Mexico, so I was fascinated with how everything was. This was the first time I had ever been out of the country too. We pulled up to a house positioned next to a row of other houses. His whole family lived on the same street.

We got out of the car and he knocked on the door. His mother was surprised to see him. She looked as if she had seen a ghost. She quickly embraced him as she cried. Next, he hugged all of his family. It was so beautiful to see.

I loved Mexico. I loved walking on the cobblestone street while looking up at a clear blue sky every day. I loved walking to the market. How your food was always fresh. How it was so peaceful. When I realized that I had to wash my clothes by hand, I didn't seem to mind it. It made me realize how spoiled we are, and we don't even know it.

Although we spent a lot of money down there, I wasn't bothered. Everything was worth it! It had been wonderful seeing him and his family together. But we knew that we couldn't stay forever. We had to get back home.

Once we returned home, things got a little better for me, even though Josh continued to work out of town. My cousin, who did not have a place to live, moved in with us. Josh was happy with this new adjustment because it meant that I wouldn't be home alone anymore.

During this same time, I took my daughter's father back to court. Things had continued to escalate to the point that he was now throwing garbage into our yard. No, I didn't have any proof, but I knew it had to be him. Who else would do something like that? Greg's tricks did not work in his favor this time, the court ruled in my favor. Now he would only have her three weekends a month. It felt so good to have my baby girl back home.

Life started to feel good again. I was even working out again with my cousin after she started to call me fat. I became proud of myself when I started to lose a little bit of weight. Josh and I started going on dates again, now that my cousin was there and able to babysit the kids for us. He even started to be at home more because he started working closer.

We still continued to argue over small things. Josh would get upset if he came home and found the house cleaned but the bed not made. If dinner wasn't all done, there was a problem. He would take it upon himself to make his own eggs, beans, and tortillas. On one occasion, I became livid because I was almost done cooking. I became spiteful and dumped salt in his beans and eggs when he walked away. He didn't realize what I had done until he took a bite of his food. He was pissed off. He would look at me and start screaming that I was lazy, along with whatever else he wanted to say.

I was at the point that I didn't care about what Josh had to say. My cousin was there with me. I had someone to spend time with. Unfortunately, she didn't stay with us that long. I came home one day, and she was just gone. No explanation. I knew that something was wrong. It wasn't like her to leave like that. But I thought maybe she wanted to move in with the boyfriend whom she would go hang out with and go clubbing with.

I still asked her whether she was okay. My husband kept asking why she had left. I felt something was strange. However, she said that things were fine, so I believed her.

It was Josh and I's wedding anniversary. I went to the city to buy a new outfit. By the time I came home, my husband was drunk like I had never seen him before. I was so angry that he had gotten so drunk around the kids. I was also angry because we had planned to go out to celebrate. I told him I was going to go anyways. He said he just needed to sleep for a little while, and then he would wake up and come meet me. I was fine with that. I went to the bar with my friends while a babysitter stayed at the house and babysat my kids. That night my husband never came.

While I was still at the bar, I got a text message from the babysitter saying that her dad was coming to pick her up. I asked her if she was okay, she said, "yeah." As I read her text, I got this feeling like something was odd. When I finally got home it was either 3 or 4 the next morning. I went right to bed. I was tired, drunk, and my feet were hurting.

When I woke up to get my phone, I had a bunch of missed calls and text messages from the babysitter. I started to read them. I could not believe what I saw. The first message said, "your husband tried to touch me in the living room." I sat up in a panic while holding back the tears. I immediately called her. She was only 15 years old at the time. She was innocent. She sat on the phone crying as she told me what happened. I couldn't believe it!

In that moment, my world came crashing down. I knew she wasn't lying. I threw on some clothes. As soon as I reached him, I started pushing and slapping him, while throwing things at him. My children were in the yard crying and screaming. "How could you?" I screamed. "The underaged babysitter? how could you?" as I punched him left and right while crying.

He looked so surprised. He said, "what do you mean?" while crying himself. He said he would never. He kept saying, "I didn't do anything." He said that he was really drunk, and that he was smoking those cigars from Mexico. He actually had the nerve to say that maybe there was something inside of them. He insisted that he would never hurt her, that he loved her, and that he was sorry as he fell to his knees crying. I continued to cry.

He went to meet with her my dad. I don't know the extent of the conversation, but I know that he wasn't allowed over there anymore. He came back and he asked me if I was willing to leave everything behind and go live in Mexico with him. I knew in that instant that he knew exactly what he had done.

I couldn't believe that I had married a monster. I found out almost 10 years later that my cousin had moved out because he kept trying to look at her in the shower, and watched her as she was changing. I couldn't believe that he was so bold to do these things right under my nose. My cousin told me that any time I was at work, he would try to lay on top of her. When he took her driving, he would try to kiss her. That's the real reason why she moved out.

I asked her why she didn't tell me back then. She said she didn't know if I would have believed her. I was disgusted with him. Who was this monster?

I told him that I was done. His actions had put a big wedge in between us. I couldn't look at him the same way. There was no coming back from this. Anytime he was home, I would leave. I went from having my own house, to sleeping at my friend's house on the couch. At this time, I started to drink a lot. I told him that I wanted to get a divorce. He continued saying that he was sorry. I didn't care because sorry wouldn't cut it for what he had done. I felt betrayed. All of my trust and faith that I had put in his hands was now gone.

I started working at a pizza place. I needed to save up enough money so that my friend and I could get an apartment together. I couldn't share the house any longer with Josh. I was disgusted with him. I hated him. I felt as though the life I lived with him was a lie.

Everything that I worked hard for had crumbled. I tried to be a good wife to him, but it was never good enough. I couldn't understand why he would come into my life and bring so much damage. Why would he hurt the ones that I loved.

I allowed it to destroy me. I started hanging with this group of girls. All we did was party. All I wanted to do was drink because of the damage he had done to me. I hadn't realized that what I had found out about this monster was nothing compared to what I would find out years later.

CHAPTER 15:
THE PINK HOUSE & PROSTITUTION

I was losing everything. But there was no way that I was going to be with a man like Josh. Thankfully, my friend wanted to get an apartment together. I was honestly a little uneasy because I knew she'd never kept her job for very long. To ease my feelings, I wanted to get something affordable, just in case my fears became a reality. We found a privately owned Pepto-Bismol-pink, two-bedroom, 1-bathroom, duplex. My friend kept saying that she wanted to get something bigger, but I talked her into agreeing to rent the pink house instead. I told her we could stack up our money for about a year, and then we could go our separate ways. I was so relieved that she agreed with me.

Upon moving in, I took most of the furniture from the house I shared with Josh while he was at work. That evening, he came home to an empty house. I didn't care because I had become heartless towards him.

My friend and I agreed that the kids would share the big bedroom, and we would share the small bedroom. We would alternate sleeping on the couch. This worked out perfectly because we were thick as thieves. We did everything together. If you saw her, you saw me as well. She was one of my best friends.

Having a roommate helped me to easily transition to being on my own with my three children. I was relieved. One of my biggest fears was having to struggle again after knowing what it was like to not live that way. Thankfully, it was extremely easy for us to pay the bills. We both were making pretty good money. On top of my paychecks, I had child support coming in.

Things in my life were going in the right direction, until we both got fired. We were upset and couldn't believe it. We were loyal to them. I was stressed out! Luckily, I quickly got another job. But it was only part-time, and it didn't even come close to the amount of money that I was making before. Now, bills were tight. I hated it! I was desperate to make money. I wasn't prepared to live from paycheck to paycheck.

One day, I got this bright idea. I knew that my friend was a self-proclaimed "ho," who slept around a lot. I somehow convinced her that we should just sell our bodies. To justify it, I told her, "you do it anyways, you might as well make some money off of it." I wasn't surprised when she said, "you're right," because she slept around a lot, to the point that it shocked me. After thinking about it for a couple of days, we got dressed really cute one night and embarked on our new journey.

We were so nervous. We gave ourselves nicknames and purchased a fake gun to keep in our bag. We set our prices, which were extremely low. We knew it, but we really didn't care. We were just trying to make some extra money.

That first night was a little weird. We didn't know where to go, so we kind of just walked around downtown which was a complete ghost town. As soon as we were about to give up, two men walked up to us, one older and one a little bit younger, and asked us why we were there. They followed it up by asking if we wanted to drink. I knew that this was our way in.

We immediately started flirting. He then asked us if we were there for sex. We said, "sure, where's all the guys at?" He let us know that they were in the country. He told us that it was kind of hard to get out there, but offered to take us. Of course, he wanted sex for free. We thought about it for a minute and we did it!

As we pulled up to where the men were in the country, I noticed there were about five or six large run down houses with big fans and old cars parked everywhere. There were different groups of men huddled up by the fire. This was our chance to do what we came to do. We got out of the car, turned up the music and we started to dance on each other. The men immediately turned their attention away from the fire towards us until they were in arms reach. One by one they started to grab us and take us to different places to have sex with us.

Even though this was our first night, we came prepared with our own blankets and condoms. We also had a silly little rule like no kissing, no going over your time, or it was going to cost more money. One by one, each man climbed on the top of us.

As each man penetrated me, one after the other, I lay there emotionless. I had no feeling at all. I just wanted them to hurry up and finish. I was disconnected to what was going on. The only thought that ran briefly across my mind was, "this is where life landed me, with strange men laying on the top of me." The houses were disgusting, and the experiences were also. We lay there as strange men's sweat dripped on us as they breathed heavily. It's something I'll honestly never forget.

On our way back home, we literally just laughed as we counted all of the money we had made. We talked about how easy it was for us. My plan had worked! As a result, we decided that that night would be the first of many.

Our routine was broken one night when a man got a hotel room instead of just having his way with us in the back of one of the broke down cars, or in one of the dirty houses. We could tell that he was really nervous. He wanted both of us. I told him to put his money down while he went into the bathroom. I didn't know if he was trying to back out of it, so I told my friend to grab all of the money and put it in a bag. Once he came out of the bathroom, he looked at us and asked about the money. We didn't know what he was going to do, or what to expect. Yes, we had the fake gun with us, but we knew that it really wasn't going to help us. Instead of sticking around to see what he was going to do, we quickly left the hotel room. We knew that something was off about him. It was only by the grace of God we never got hurt.

We had no remorse at all. I didn't care about what we had just done. My only thought was how stupid could these men be!

Shortly after that, the tables turned. We went out for another night, but this night we found a different camp to go to. For whatever reason, at the end of the night, I left my handbag behind. All of the money that I had made was gone. I was so angry. I couldn't believe I had been that stupid and careless.

The news that girls were going to the country campgrounds selling their bodies had spread like wildfire. One day, out of the blue, my husband called me immediately after it had gotten to him. Without hesitation, he asked me if it had been me. I nonchalantly lied to him by saying, "no, why would I do that?" Despite the fact that I knew he had believed me, or at least it appeared that way, I was concerned that if he had heard, most likely the police had also. There was no way that I would continue and risk getting arrested. It wasn't that serious. It was something that we did for some extra money, so we decided to stop, and we never really talked about it again.

A little while after we made our decision to stop selling our bodies, my friend got involved with another man and moved out pretty quickly. I was very glad that I had made the decision to get something that I could afford. My rent was $550. Sadly, because I never spent my money wisely, I struggled to pay the rent. However, my landlord ended up knocking my rent down to $350 because he said I was a good mom.

During this time, Josh and I came up with a verbal agreement concerning custody. He started paying me child support, paying for daycare for the boys, and giving me a little bit of cash every month. He even picked up all three of my children. You would have thought that I had it made, but I didn't.

I was living my worst nightmare. The one that I told Josh that I never wanted to live when he asked to have a child years prior. I was struggling, despite the fact that I received as much child support as I could, worked part time, and received money from whatever government assistance program I would qualify for. I still couldn't handle everything. I became even more bitter!

Truthfully, it was my fault that I was in the situation that I was in financially. I wasted so much money on clothes and shoes. Honestly, I never even desired to want better out of life during that time. I never thought about my future. I had little to no drive. I had grown used to just surviving. As long as my lights were on, and my kids had food and some new sneakers on their feet, I didn't complain.

But what I did do was drink. I started drinking at least a bottle of wine a day. Every day after work, I went directly to the store for a bottle of wine. As soon as I got home, I drank it as I sat on my front porch watching my kids play.

At that time, I didn't realize what I was doing to myself. I had no idea what path I was heading down. Honestly, I didn't care. . .

CHAPTER 16: WILD WOMAN

I was working a part-time job cleaning a hotel on a military base. I was broken. I was stuck facing the fact that my marriage didn't work. As a result, I stopped trusting men. All I wanted to do was party. Someway, somehow, I managed to connect with a circle of women who wanted the same thing.

Together, we would do family things with the kids, like go to the movies, or the pool. Then we would party. Our lives were mostly surrounded by drinking and men. And I loved every moment of it.

I had never been single out in the world. My relationship with my daughter's father started when I was a teenager. After that relationship dissolved, I got into a relationship with Josh, got married, and had two more children—all while I was still young.

The freedom that I was now experiencing caused me to become wild. For the first time, nobody was telling me what I could and couldn't do anymore. There was no one telling me what I could and couldn't wear. Who I could and couldn't talk to. Or even what time I had to be home.

I started passing out my number like it was free candy. I talked to a lot of different men at one time, and didn't feel like there was anything wrong with it either. Every morning, I would pick up my phone and text 10 to 15 guys, "good morning," as well as send them the same picture of myself. This became a thrill for me.

During this time, Josh was still very upset. He still struggled with the fact that I would never be with him again. He was also mad because I was going out. But I didn't care. As far as I was concerned, he could get as upset with me as he wanted. He was the one who caused all of this!

My husband would tell me to come back home. He would say I left him because I wanted to party, or that I didn't want to have a family anymore. This was far from the truth and he knew it. I left because he touched the underaged babysitter. I was going to do whatever the heck I wanted to do from now on. I was going to wear whatever I wanted, and drink however much I wanted. In some sick way, I saw it as me punishing him. Nobody was going to stop me.

I stayed in the streets. I always thought that I would miss something if I were at home. I had no desire to be home. I was that girl who was at the club Wednesday, Friday, Saturday, and sometimes at a house party during the week. I literally drank every single day to the point that without realizing it, I had become codependent.

When I went out, I liked the attention that I started getting. I had never had that much attention in my life. I craved it. It's all that I cared about. I had to keep getting it too. It became like a drug to me. To keep getting the high that I needed, I wore the most revealing clothing. Dresses that barely came under my butt. I wore no bra with everything see-through mesh. Every time I danced, my whole butt would be out, and I didn't even care. I would laugh and just pull my dress back down. I was that crazy girl, who walked around the bar with no shoes because I thought it was cute.

I would go to the bar broke, but would leave drunk. I literally became a man eater. I danced on every man in the bar. I was pulled left and right by different men. Some would pick me up and throw me in the air. I would place my legs around their waist and start grinding on them. I would do the splits on men as they lay on the ground. I did this all while laughing like it was a game. Afterwards, I would get them to buy me a drink and go right to the next guy.

I would focus on a couple guys. Like clockwork, I'd walk past them and tell them that they smelled nice. I did this as I touched their arm. Knowing I got their attention, I would go sit down and wait for them to come up to me. Without fail, it worked like a charm every single time.

Although I was extremely flirtatious, I wasn't sleeping around at this point. I was just getting free drinks in the bar. I had so many men who thought I was beautiful. I knew that they were just in love with my body. They probably didn't think I was even beautiful, they just wanted to get me drunk, hoping that I would sleep with them—not knowing that I wasn't. I was more focused on spending their money on drinks instead of my own.

I felt as if I was now in control of my environment. I felt empowered. I wanted to be the center of attention, and I was. Because of it, I started to have a really big attitude. I would pull away from different people, walk past, and ignore them as they spoke, and I was always ready to fight and curse anyone out at the drop of a hat.

Unfortunately, my first opportunity to fight at the bar wasn't with anyone other than Josh. On that night, he showed up to the bar and watched me as I danced all over everyone. I thought it was funny. I was trying to agitate him. I wanted to hurt him. I wanted to show him what he had lost. I wanted to make him believe once and for all that I was never going back to him. To my surprise, he didn't get angry. Rather, he begged me to come home, with desperation written all over his face. I laughed and pushed him away before going outside with a guy. Once outside, I got down in the dirt on my knees in between two cars. The next thing I know, my husband comes and starts punching the guy until his wrist broke. I could not believe it!

I thought he had left. I was so enraged. I started punching him while screaming. This continued until my friends pulled me off of him. It was then that I noticed my kids were in the car watching me beat up their dad.

After that night, I started to have more violent outbursts. I would be at the bar throwing drinks on women, hitting people with my shoes, throwing chairs, and even snorting daddy bars off the bathroom counter.

I had completely gone wild! But I still managed to function when I was drinking. I never blacked out, no matter how drunk I became. I continued to keep my job. I made sure to never neglect my kids. I never allowed my daily hangovers to stop me from picking up my kids from daycare, or from making homemade dinners.

No matter how out of control I had been the night before, I felt like I was super mom. I felt like I was just "doing me" sometimes. And felt that I deserved to have fun because everybody was being taken care of.

I was so naive. I didn't realize all of the damage that I was doing to myself. I didn't know that I was really acting like this because of all of the pain that I was in. I wasn't aware that depression had caused me to go on a self-destructive path. I didn't know that driving home drunk after staying out until 5 or 6 in the morning was self-destructive. Or that having a hangover everyday was even a result of it either.

CHAPTER 17:
MR. OFFICER

Working around military men meant that I had my fair share of them. Because they were usually there for a specific time period, I only saw them 3-4 times a year for a period of 4 to 6 weeks. No matter how many of them that I had been involved with, I, like everyone else, had my favorites text me right before they got back. The initial conversation was the same, "did you miss me? see you soon."

I had become used to the routine of things with them. Some of the other women would go over and beyond for these men, knowing that they would only be there for a few weeks. They knew that almost everyone either already had a girlfriend, or a wife, back home, whom they were cheating on with them. It was annoying. I would sit back, and watch girls repeatedly fall in love with these men, only to be left heartbroken weeks later.

I refused to be like the other women, so I developed my own system. I knew that if a man was a certain rank, it meant that he shared a barrack with someone. Which meant that if you decided to go on back with him and have sex, you would be doing it while his roommate was asleep. I realized very fast that I did not like that, so I started asking people what rank they were before I decided that I would go back and sleep with them.

There were a couple of different men that I talked to for quite some time, even after they left. While they were in town, we would play boyfriend and girlfriend. I enjoyed every second of it too. I never cared about what situation they had back home. I knew that I was just having fun. I never brought anybody who was temporary around my children. While my "boyfriends" were in town, I'd drive out to the base and go see them, or only see them on the weekends while the children were at their father's house.

This is when I turned into a ho. I started sleeping with people and I didn't even know their name. What's worse is that I slept with people that I knew my friends had sex with. I didn't care. I did this until I got really fed up with the "cag boys." Now, anytime I would go to the bar, the first question I asked was, "are you here for six weeks, or are you stationed here." The men started lying about the length of time they'd be in town. They knew that women, like me, were getting fed up with temporary relationships.

I wanted something more serious. I wanted to be loved. I didn't want to continuously chase these men, wondering if they were also talking to other people. Yes, I knew that I was talking to a lot of people as well. But it was only because I was lonely. I knew that nobody really cared about anything that I was going through. And no matter how much I lay snuggled up against their bodies, I was just entertainment for the night.

My desire for something more serious was finally met when I was introduced to Mr. Officer by one of my friends. Before that, I had seen him around town a couple of times. When he would see me—although we hadn't been formally introduced—he'd call me "little lady." He was cute, stood at about six foot one, dark chocolate skin, bald-headed, with a beard, and he always smelled amazing.

Mr. Officer, and I, didn't start to really talk until the night of the Navy ball. I had gotten invited by a friend, who, at the last minute, told me that he wasn't able to get the ticket. I was really hurt and upset. I went to the bar because I knew that after the Navy Ball, everybody would show up there. Besides, I was already dressed in a deep peach v-neck spandex dress that went underneath my butt, with no bra, and a jacket that was the length of my dress.

As soon as Mr. Officer came into the bar, he told me I looked very nice. He offered to buy me a drink. Over drinks, I told him that I had gotten ditched, to which he replied, "I would have never ditched you." As we talked, I was pretty convinced that he had a girlfriend. He told me that they had broken up, and that she was moving out soon. I was a little intrigued after that night.

Whenever I went out, I started paying closer attention to him. Every time he saw me, he said that my drinks were on him. He even began to pull me away from different men. At this point, he started calling me, asking about my plans for that Friday night. He would make sure to let me know that he'll see me out.

One night while out, I saw him walking to the bar with his "girlfriend." As they sat next to each other, another lady walked into the bar. I could tell by the reaction of others in the bar that they were shocked. I asked my friend what was going on. She then told me that the woman who had just walked in was his wife! Wife? I said, "what do you mean? why is he sitting next to this other woman?" I was confused as I watched the wife walk straight to the back and start shooting pool with her friends. Then she walks up to Mr. Officer, gets his debit card, orders him a drink, hands them both to him, and then walks off. I was so confused. I thought, "this is not how a marriage is supposed to be." My friend then told me that they're separated. I was like, here we go again! This seemed to be the norm for military families.

That night, Mr. Officer had been messaging me. I told him I didn't want to get involved in anything like that. He assured me that him and his girlfriend were done, and that she was leaving soon. He assured me that I didn't have anything to worry about. He then started explaining the dynamic of his and his wife's situation. He said it was easier to stay together for the children because of all the moving. He said that he had his own bedroom, and he was free to do whatever he wanted, and she was also free, and if any of them ever got really serious with somebody, then they would get divorced. He followed that with he had never found anyone serious enough for him to pursue divorce.

I should have stopped messaging him, but I didn't. Mr. Officer was a smooth talker. He told me to trust him; "daddy" wasn't coming into my life to hurt me. He started calling me pumpkin. From that point on, he started popping in and out of work saying hi, calling me just to hear my voice, even bringing me food. He would even come and sit and talk to me as I worked out. He started asking about my children and buying them clothes.

Seeing him, quickly became an everyday thing. I finally felt comfortable enough to bring him around my children, even though the first time was an accident because they came home early. Like a natural, he started playing with them, giving them nicknames, and even helping me parent. To my surprise, my children instantly loved him!

Mr. Officer spent time with not only me, but with them. He helped them do their homework and everything while I was in the kitchen making dinner. I was so shocked in the beginning because he spent so much time with them. When he wasn't with us, we spent hours on the phone texting back and forth. He always sent me love songs. Because of him I fell in love with Anthony Hamilton and Lyfe Jennings. I would cook while listening to those songs, as I waited until he came over to cuddle with my babies on the other side of the couch. For the first time in a long time, I was happy again. I never felt good enough just being by myself and single. I realize that I had to be validated by a man. I lived my life like that for many years.

Although things had been going well with Mr. Officer and I, things were not perfect. There had been signs that some things were not adding up. However, whenever I'd question him about them, I was left feeling as though I was tripping.

Even though he spent a lot of time with my children, I never really saw his. The way that I saw the situation, since we were together, it was only right that I get to know them too. I questioned him about it because it just didn't feel right. Another area of concern for me was the fact that his wife was driving his car. One day, as I was driving his truck, I saw his car coming towards me. I went to wave and it was his wife. I called him and let him know. To which he would say, "I'll handle the situation."

I believed everything that man told me, to the point that it was like I didn't have a brain of my own. I was extremely loyal. He would tell me things like, "if I'm yours, prove it." I posted pictures of the two of us; posted pictures of me and his hats or his jacket or whatever. No matter how much I tried to prove myself to him, he wouldn't get a divorce. He kept using the fact that I was still legally married as an excuse as to why he wasn't getting a divorce. He would remind me that he spent a lot of time at my house. Mr. Officer kept saying things like, "you have me, why are you complaining?" Or, "it's just a piece of paper." Afterwards, he would grab my face and kiss me with all this passion, and say, "I love you." I would shut up about it for a couple of months.

Mr. Officer was very strategic; he constantly said that we were his priority and he showed it. The first year we were together was great. I saw him almost every day; he spent some nights and weekends with me, and checked up on the children regularly. He even helped me get whatever I needed for my children.

But then things changed. He began to tell me that I was his property. That nobody else could have me. He made it very clear that there was no more dancing all over everybody and partying like I had been. He even told me that I had to follow his rules because he liked things a certain way. It should have been a red flag when he called me his "property," but it wasn't. At the time, I didn't care. I actually liked the fact that he claimed me.

When disrespectful men would come up to me while we were out, he would tell them that I'm off limits. He would flick his wrist and shew them away. Although he was very metro (you know the type of man that waxes his eyebrows, is meticulous about his appearance, and gets his feet done), he was extremely bold and aggressive towards them. He would tell them, don't let this soft voice fool you. When they would try to argue with him, he carelessly laughed in their faces. A lot of people were confused because they knew that he was married, and couldn't understand why he was claiming me so openly.

As I watched him disrespect men, I didn't think there was anything wrong with it. Each time, I sat quietly at his side and let him handle things. In my mind, he was just protecting me because I was his.

Unfortunately, without noticing the disrespect turned towards me. On one particular night, he told me to go to the bar, but I wasn't allowed to drink. I sat watching everybody else drinking and getting drunk. I was bored and really annoyed because I wanted to drink. Mr. Officer pointed out those who were drunk and told me that I looked like them when I drank. He went on to say that I needed to control myself. That I didn't need to be in the bar walking around with no shoes on, or have my butt out while I was dancing.

I was appalled. But I sat there listening. He told me that I needed to sit my monkey butt down sometimes, and stop being in everybody's face because it wasn't a good look. I couldn't believe what I was hearing from him. Mr. Officer went on to say he wasn't going to have a woman who did that type of stuff. And that I couldn't wear anything that was too revealing.

After that night, things between us changed drastically. He no longer treated me the same way. Whenever I was going out, he questioned me about what I was wearing. There were times that I had to send him pictures of my outfit. As if that weren't enough, when he was in arms reach, he would walk right up to me and grab my vagina and say that others didn't need to see it through my leggings. At first, I thought this was cute. Until he continued to do it and made me change.

Mr. Officer really started to treat me like his property when he became extremely possessive. He started to act like a dictator. He would get mad and throw fits about the way I wore my hair and makeup. I would change it to his liking because I wanted nothing more than to please him.

Whenever he called, and I didn't answer right away, he would unleash his fury on me. He would come to my house just to argue with me and check my phone. To appease him, I had to have my phone on 24-7. This included during the time that I was sleeping.

Slowly, I began to change to accommodate him and did the things that he wanted. In the beginning, I felt like everything he said made sense. Like a programmed robot, I started calling him whenever I left the house, and when I returned. I checked in with him while on my lunch breaks. I literally let him know my every move. At the time, it didn't bother me to do it because that was my man. I thought it was just a respectful thing to do.

Even though I did what he asked, it was not enough. I became frustrated with him. No matter how much I insisted, he wouldn't get a divorce from his wife. As a result, there had been times when he asked me to lie to his chain of command if I received a call asking about our relationship. I was directed to say that nothing had been going on, we were just best friends. I was confused! But he covered his tracks by telling me that he could be kicked out of the military because cheating on your spouse was not allowed or tolerated. And that he worked too hard for his career to be thrown away. He guilted me into going along with him by telling me that if I loved him, I would do it.

I knew his career was important to him. I did love him. So I was willing to lie for him, even though I didn't understand everything. After everything blew over, he told me that his wife had become really jealous of our relationship. Mr. Officer claimed that out of everyone that he had ever dated, she knew that he was serious about me. Because there was now the possibility that she could lose everything, she started trouble.

I started not to believe him. There had been so many times in the relationship with him that I knew that things didn't add up. As naive as I was at times, I knew that two plus two did not equal five. I felt in my gut that something was always off with what he was saying. Instead of going with my intuition, I just believed him, because I didn't want to be that argumentative girlfriend.

In the middle of me dealing with him and his drama, I had no clue what was going on around me. My children were still going back and forth to their father's house. The boy's father would pick them up after school, since he got off of work before me. If my daughter wasn't with her dad that weekend, she would go with the boys. This meant that I never had my kids on the weekend. I never felt like there was an issue with it either because I had my kids Monday through Friday, unless there was some schedule change.

During one of the weeks that I had my children, when I got out of the shower while they watched cartoons, I went into the living room and caught my daughter acting out sexually. I lost my mind. I couldn't believe what I was seeing. Without thinking, I started screaming at the top of my lungs, while cussing and spanking her. I said things to her that I should have never said.

After sitting back for a minute, I grabbed her and asked her where she learned that from. I asked her, "who hurt you?" I began to fall apart. Because of the way I initially reacted, she was now scared of me. In response to my question, she kept saying, "nobody, nobody." I was a mess. I begged her to tell me, but she kept telling me, "I don't know where I learned it from, I don't know," until she completely shut down.

I was a wreck and bawling. She was crying too. I didn't know what to do. As we went to a church member's family's house, with three of my friends and their children, I continued to question her. I named different people, but she kept saying, "no." I was desperate at this point. I needed to find out who had done something to my baby. The worst thing that could have happened to my daughter happened.

I felt so guilty for the way that I spanked her. Whatever happened, wasn't her fault. My mind was racing as we drove out of town that day. As we passed by the boys' dad's house, something inside of me said it was him. I immediately reacted. I quickly pulled my car into his driveway, my friends followed behind. I jumped out of the car like a bat out of hell and started banging on his door, as I screamed, "what did you do to my child." He opened the door, but left his big metal screen door closed. I was punching it as he looked shocked. I had seen this look of guilt on his face before.

He kept saying, "what are you talking about? No, no." I began to scream louder as I banged on the screen door. I started kicking the screen door. I had on sandals, but didn't care about injuring my foot. That day, I felt a strength that I had never felt before. My only thought was that that door had to come down!

My friends stood back screaming at him. As he denied doing anything, they screamed, "you know exactly what you did." Suddenly my foot went through the screen door. There had been a big metal pole near. I didn't hesitate to pick it up like I was a gladiator. I drove the pole through the door with one arm. It hit him repeatedly until he fell on the ground holding his leg.

I kept saying the same thing over and over again, "I'm going to kill you." My children sat in the car screaming as they watched in horror. All of a sudden, not knowing why, I stopped unleashing my fury on him, I got back in the car with my kids.

My daughter became really tight-lipped about it after that. I tried to get her dad to go and kill him, but he wouldn't. I took her to the police station, but because she wouldn't say anything, they couldn't do anything. I was so angry and felt so hopeless. I had always taught her that nobody was allowed to touch her body parts. I made sure she wore leggings under her dresses. I didn't leave my children with anyone random. My children couldn't even go in their bedrooms and shut the door.

I started going over things in my head. I realized that I had missed so many signs. She had started wetting the bed out of the blue. She told me that she couldn't walk and didn't want to run anymore. There was even a time that she didn't want to go to his house anymore. I thought she was just being a brat. I even told her to stop being that way and to go to her dad. All while he stood at the door begging her to go with him.

I felt so much shame and guilt. I felt so much disbelief. What happened to my baby? I tried to ask her different ways what had happened, but she would never tell me. But she did say that the boys were safe. Even though I didn't know, because she wouldn't tell me, I bent down to her level and told her that nobody was ever going to hurt her again. And that she was never going to go back to his house again. There was nothing I could do about the boys going back. I couldn't prove that he had done anything to her. And when questioned, the boys acted like they were fine.

Josh wasn't allowed to come to my house. Whenever I saw him, I threw rocks at him, and called him a rapist. I called him a child molester. I did this out in the open. I didn't care either. He wasn't fazed at all. He would look at me and laugh, as I acted like a wild woman in the street.

I was lost. I felt hopeless, so I started to drink a lot. I lost faith in so many people around this time. I didn't want my daughter out of my sight. Although I no longer sent her to Josh's house, he gained access to her through her father. They became close friends. I was pissed off. I called her father, yelling as I asked him, "why are you hanging out with the man who put his d**k in my daughter's mouth? how could you?" I told him he did something to your daughter. He never believed me. He would just tell me that I was crazy and that it didn't happen, I made it up. I was furious. Why would I make something like that up?

I was sick about everything that was going on. I felt helpless. Josh went camping with them. Greg invited him over to his house to watch a boxing match. The predator was able to keep his filthy eyes on my baby. I felt like he was taunting my daughter. Instead of giving up, I kept screaming at Greg, until he finally stopped hanging out with him.

I went to church after everything happened and was in a daze. All kinds of thoughts ran through my mind. I sat there, really mad at God. I couldn't understand why he would let something like that happen to my baby. That day, I must have looked how I felt because everyone knew that something was wrong with me. My pastor even asked if something was wrong. I told him that I hated God. In response, he said, "He's not the one who did it!" I didn't understand what he meant by that. To me, God was the one with the power to stop it, and he didn't. After that, I didn't go to church for a long time. I even lost the little faith that I had been holding on to.

I was a wreck. I was hopeless. I cried often. I felt so heavy and extremely low. This was the first time that I wanted to commit suicide. I was emotionally dead, as I tried to comprehend why I didn't see the signs. I hated my life. I was trying to hold a job. Trying to be strong and not break down and cry in front of my daughter.

Unfortunately, all that I was going through didn't stop me from being wrapped up in Mr. Officer. Although it became hard to have sex with him. While trying to be intimate with him, I kept picturing my child. It was too much for me to bear, so I started to drink Grey Goose vodka before sex. Sex not only freaked me out, it grossed me out.

My boyfriend now acted as if he was tired of the drama. So he decided we were just going to start going to the city for dates. The truth was he was trying to hide us from his wife. The only thing he had grown tired of was everybody running their mouth about us.

I had become a notorious side chick. I was a home wrecking woman, who had become wrapped up in everything that he said. Nobody could tell me anything different. He was my man. He was perfect in my eyes. And I thought proving my love and fighting for us was normal.

Initially, I didn't see anything wrong with me and his wife both being at his sporting events. I wasn't concerned that she looked at me crazy every time she saw me. Or that she ran up on me at one of his basketball games after he had gotten hurt screaming, "why are you here?"

After a while, I started questioning him more and more. Especially after I got a phone call from his ex-girlfriend telling me to be careful. With more evidence mounting up, proving that he was lying to me all along, I started to feel lonely again. I started to realize that the only thing that I was being used for was sex. I even started hearing rumors that he was cheating on me. Which I knew to be true because he was no longer around like he used to be. And he started to check out and flirt with other women in my presence.

The straw that broke the camel's back was a trip he had taken to Las Vegas, Nevada. I had no idea that his wife was going with him. I was surprised to see pictures of them on Facebook. Seeing them together without their children made me realize that everything he had told me for the last two years was a lie. I called and texted him, but he never responded.

That night, I decided to go and have sex with someone else. I felt like giving my body to another man was the perfect way to get even with him. I decided that I would play his game instead of breaking up with him. I was no longer going to be his property. I wanted to be my own person.

Mr. Officer denied that anything happened on his trip with his wife. He made up some bogus story about him wanting to have a threesome with his wife and another woman, to which she wouldn't agree. I couldn't believe him. But I could never stay mad at him. The truth is that I was addicted to him and to sex with him.

It was difficult for me to walk away from him for good. No matter how much wrong he had done, I would end up begging him to not break up with me. I was weak, and thought my life was nothing without him. I was willing to do anything that he asked me to do.

I had become brainwashed. He made me believe that I talked too much. That I complained too much. He told me that he "just wanted a b**** that would listen." So I started to be more quiet. But that didn't work. He would purposely start fights with me only to make me look like a fool. He would embarrass me in front of other people by screaming at me while they laughed. They would try to talk some sense into me by telling me to leave him alone, he didn't want me anymore. That was far from the truth. Following each explosive episode was an apology and hours of makeup sex.

I don't know if it was because I became tired of the toxic cycle that I was stuck in, but I started to talk to other people. I pushed boundaries with other men. But I always tried to cover my tracks by deleting messages. I even started to go out without telling him. This didn't work because he would show up there, or send me pictures of myself. He knew everywhere that I would go because he had people everywhere.

Feeling trapped, I tried to break up with Mr. Officer. I was tired of being controlled. I was tired of the lies. No matter how I tried to get away from him, I couldn't. He told me that he wasn't done with me and he wasn't going anywhere. He would send me pictures of him sitting on my couch when I wasn't home. He had gained entry by climbing through the window.

I quickly realized it wasn't going to be easy for me to break things off with him, so I stopped trying. I continued to go along with things, even after his wife confronted me as I was coming out of the nail salon. She questioned me about my relationship with him. I lied and said that we were just friends, but she knew that it wasn't true. She told me that he was lying about me. I didn't understand that at the time.

Of course, he denied everything. He even told me that he was ready to get a divorce from her, and that I needed to go forward with mine. So I did. I sat down with my soon to be ex-husband at Dairy Queen and filled out the papers. We submitted them and were divorced in 4 days.

Mr. Officer lied to me and said that we would get married. He sold me a fairytale when he told me that I would move everywhere with him. We talked about him having his vasectomy reversed and having children together. Everything seemed so real. But they weren't.

Mr. Officer was the master of manipulation. He showed me divorce papers. I found out later that they were fake. Apparently, his wife wanted a divorce and he freaked out and told her no. You would have thought that this all was enough to make me leave him alone for good, but it wasn't.

Everything in me told me to leave this man alone, but I fought against it. I kept trying to convince myself that it would all work out.

For whatever reason, I never wanted to fully believe that he had been lying to me for all those years.

The situation between Mr. Officer and I started to weigh heavy on me. To the point that I was sick. Everything was screaming against this relationship, but I wouldn't listen. The Spirit of the Lord even cried out against it. During the turmoil, I went to church and was prophesied to, and told to not let that man move into my house. But I ignored what was spoken and did so anyway.

As soon as I made the decision to disobey the voice of the Lord, things started to get worse. While we were out dancing, I ended up grabbing this woman he had been dancing all over. He and I started yelling and screaming at each other as we walked out of the casino extremely drunk. Suddenly, he grabbed me by the neck, picked me up, and dangled me over a nearby rail. I attempted to release his hands from around my neck by gripping his wrist. I could hear the onlookers saying, "he's choking her, he's choking her." Thankfully, he let me down. But continued to threaten to leave me in the city with no way to get home.

I couldn't let him leave without me. I had given him my debit card and driver's license to hold for me while we were having drinks at the bar. He tried to outrun me to reach the car first. I ran after him crying and screaming. We finally make it to the car, and I get in. We yelled at each other until he stopped yelling back. I couldn't stop yelling at him though. I couldn't believe how he did me over another woman. I cocked back and hit him on the right side of his face a few times as he yelled for me to stop. When I wouldn't, he backhanded me and busted my lip.

I let out the ugliest loudest cry ever. He pulled over and threatened to leave me on the side of the freeway. He screamed at me, and attempted to drag me out of the car. He finally stopped. I sat there crying as I held my face. Instead of taking me home, he dropped me off at my friend's house. As soon as she saw me, she said, "let's call the police." I refused. I kept telling her that I punched him first. I knew that they would believe him over me because he was a Navy policeman.

I was beyond hurt. I told Mr. Officer that I was done with him. I thought I meant it. But as soon as he came over to get me, he walked right in and picked me up like a baby and took me home. Once there, he made love to me. I thought, "this isn't what I wanted. I wanted to be done." My body on the other hand was screaming yes to him kissing me where he had just smacked me. He apologized over and over again. I gave in.

The next thing I knew, I found myself stuck in this domestic abuse cycle with him. I always blamed myself because I was the one who always hit him first. Things went from him just yelling and screaming at me, and maybe pushing some things around, to this. I always thought that if I had never put my hands on him first, then the physical abuse would not have happened.

Fortunately, no matter how we acted towards each other, whenever the kids were around, he played nice. He was literally a completely different person.

As everything was happening, I wanted nothing to do with him. I couldn't understand why he wouldn't go home. I wanted him to leave me alone after we would get into arguments. But he wouldn't unless he was in the mood to block me from calling him for a couple of days.

Mr. Office became extremely insecure. Because of it, I never knew what to expect. In the middle of the night, he came home, grabbed both of my ankles, and yanked me out of the bed. My body went over the wooden footboard before my head made contact with it. I sat on the floor crying as I held my head. I couldn't understand why I was being woken up like that. I was scared. He yelled for me to give him my phone to check. I couldn't believe the nightmare I was now living.

The next morning, I discovered that he had taken my rent money. I called him crying as I begged for him to give it back. After telling me no several times, and hanging up on me, he finally told me to meet him by the racetrack with some snacks. I did exactly as he asked. I needed to get my rent money back. After walking around the racetrack for quite some time, pretending to be in love, he gave me my rent money back, and told me that he would be over later that night.

I should have left him then, but I didn't. As a result, the fights continued and got worse. One fight in particular left everything in the house turned upside down. As we screamed and yelled at each other, I threw things at him as I was getting pushed and shoved all over the house. This continued until he started dragging me by my feet out of the house as I screamed and cried. He threatened to stomp my face in, called me all out of my name, as he shouted about being from New York. This went on until the last next-door neighbor came out and yelled for him to stop, or she was going to call the police. He picked up a rock and threw it at her as he said, "I am the police, b****." I crawled back into the house and cried.

After each fight, he always had a way of making me feel as though it was all my fault. I started to believe that I must have been in the wrong. I must have overreacted. I would tell him that I was sorry.

Things started to take a toll on me physically. Because of the stress, my body was weak. I was losing weight like crazy. I either couldn't sleep, or all I wanted to do was sleep. I got massive migraines. My hair started falling out. I had spots throughout my hair where I was bald. I was left asking myself "how did I let it get this far?" I couldn't understand why I even wanted him to be my husband. I realized that there was no way I could deal with this for the rest of my life. I felt so used up and washed out. I didn't believe that anyone else would love me.

I finally caught him cheating. I had just left the grocery store and was driving past this little Mexican store. There he was leaning up against another woman. I couldn't believe it. I ran in the store and started screaming. The girl smirked at me while he acted like he had no clue why I was upset. He laughed. I walked out of the store, found his car, poured the gallon of milk on it, and smashed the muffin mix everywhere and left.

After this incident, things continued to get worse until I told him to take his stuff and leave me alone. Before he did, I found out that he never left his wife. She actually left to be closer to his next duty station. Randomly, one day, I got a phone call from her. She was laughing on the other end. After we talked, she asked me how it felt to be cheated on, before hanging up. Shortly after this, he left me and the other woman, and moved on to be with his wife.

Although he left, we continued to communicate. He told me we were going to work things out. I believed him when he bought the plane tickets for me to visit him. I was excited. I was with him for two weeks. I really thought we would be together, until one of his new girlfriends called me telling me to leave her man alone. She knew details about me and my children that could only come from him. He had the nerve to tell her that I was pathetic and only needed him for money.

But even after that, I continued to talk to him. He even came to visit us. But I knew that things were different between us. We were strangers. He went back to the island that he was now stationed at. And I was left with the realization that everything I had known for the last three years was now over.

I felt a sigh of relief and sadness. Who was I going to check in with? At that moment, I felt alone. I felt unloved. He left me broken. I was bitter. I was an emotional wreck. I was a good woman that kept dancing with the devil! I was never supposed to be entertaining him. God is never going to send you someone else's husband.

CHAPTER 18:
CUSTODY

My baby brother whom I had only met once, didn't grow up in foster care like me and my other brother. He was raised by his biological father instead. Although he was with his father, it still wasn't the ideal situation because his father was involved in gangs and drugs. And there were a lot of women coming in and out of their house.

One day, Marcel called me crying from a safe haven. He had just been shot at. But he didn't want to live in the safe haven. Without hesitation, I offered my home to him. At the time, I was still living in the pink townhouse. I decided that he could sleep on the couch.

The little town we lived in was nothing like Las Vegas. I let him know that the stuff he was doing there would not be tolerated. Here, he didn't have to worry about gang banging. He had a real chance to turn his life around. I was relieved when he responded to what I had to say with excitement.

His father finally signed over temporary rights to me. I drove down to Vegas with my male friend to pick up my brother. As soon as I got him, I let him know that I was not going to be the cool sister anymore. I had rules that he had to follow. I was only 26 years old trying to now raise a teenager.

In the beginning, everything was great. I got him a little cheap boost mobile phone, a bunch of clothes, and a haircut. I was trying to set him up to go in the right direction too. I introduced him to successful black men who had come out of the gang life—who changed their life around completely. I thought it would be a good thing for him to be in a military town too.

Unfortunately, I hadn't considered other facts. As soon as my brother started school, there was a huge target on his back. He constantly wanted to wear red. I was already in the principal's office during the first week of school. They kept saying that he was a gang member from Compton who sells drugs. I was absolutely dumbfounded!

My brother didn't make the transition any better. Instead of telling people that what they were saying wasn't true, he went with it. I noticed he started to cause problems on purpose. I kept trying to fill his head with knowledge, despite what was going on. I reminded him that he needed a good job. I told him that he needed to finish school, so that he could make something of himself; and he could prove everybody wrong who said that he was going to be worthless.

He always responded to me like he totally understood. But his actions said something else. I was getting calls from the principal's office every other day because there was a fight, or he talked back to the teacher. He now started to add more stress upon me.

In the midst of the drama with my brother, I continued to struggle. I wasn't making enough money with the job I was working, so I picked up a side job cleaning a small dental office. Despite the fact that my brother was old enough to work, he didn't want to. At this point it wasn't a big deal because he didn't have a problem helping out with my kids. But then everything turned. He started sleeping in all day, blasting music, ditching school, and stealing my car. To top it all off, the disrespectfulness became unbelievable.

His behavior led to me talking to either the police, or probation officer, often. I wanted him to stay out of trouble, go to school, and get good grades. Instead, he started getting very infatuated with certain girls. I started hearing about him pushing and walking one girl around the school by her hair like she was some animal. I was shocked about his behavior and his lack of respect for women. I knew this stemmed from him not having his own mother in his life. And from everything he saw with random women coming in and out of his father's house.

The more I pointed him in the right direction, the more he went in the opposite direction. I couldn't understand it for the life of me. He was so bright and had so much potential. After a while, I became angry dealing with his attitude and lack of respect. We started to argue every day. I was young, and didn't know how to take care of a disrespectful teenager.

I became so lost in the process. I cried a lot. I kept feeling like I was failing him. I was trying my best. I kept telling him that he was going to cause problems with me and my kids' fathers, and something had to change. I never wanted to give up on him because I felt like everyone else had. I also didn't want my boys to start doing the things he did. But he still didn't listen.

I felt like everything around me was falling apart. Although I continued to work two jobs and take care of my kids, I never had enough money. So I started drinking more. It was embarrassing. My brother found me on the ground several times drunk out of my mind with pills. I was hopeless, and I really didn't want to live anymore. Things were hard. I felt like I never had anybody to really talk to during that time. There was no one to really understand the things that I was going through.

There was so much on my plate all at once. I was tired of everything, including the town I lived in. I had been embarrassed by my brother's behavior. I was at the end of my rope with my children's fathers. They were still trying to make my life a living hell any chance they got. I petitioned the court for permission to move to Las Vegas. At the time, I don't even know why I didn't just get up and move and then petition the court. I was only moving to another part of the state, not another state.

Nevertheless, I had a court date coming up. Before the time came, I had decided that I didn't want to move anymore. As I waited for the date to come, I ended up missing it. During that time, there had been so much going on at work. I thought court was on a different date. I ended up going to court for a child support hearing I had. When I arrived at court, I was informed by a lawyer that I had missed my court date. I was dumbfounded. I told the lawyer that I didn't miss it because it was the following week.

Panic set in when the lawyer told me that the judge ruled in Josh's favor. I was only given permission to see my kids four days out of the month. I looked at Josh as he sat on the stand. All I could say was, "you took my kids from me," as I cried out. I cried so much that I was dry heaving. I almost threw up in the courtroom. I felt so much agony.

My children were the only thing that I had in my life, and they were taken away from me. When I received the official court papers in the mail, I couldn't deny it. I had lost full custody of my children. That day, I sank to the floor screaming. I couldn't believe what I had read. I instantly filed papers trying to appeal everything. I provided documentation that I was working, letters from friends, and even from the children's school, stating that I was a good mother. Despite my efforts, nothing worked. I couldn't understand how the judge could rule the way he had. I didn't even have a criminal record.

Now I had to watch Josh and Greg work together to take away everything I loved. My children were the only things that I felt that I really had. This killed me. I went through every emotion imaginable. I felt like my children were dead, like I had lost them forever. I felt like I had lost the only reason why I didn't commit suicide. I couldn't believe that they had been taken away from the person who had been most consistent in their lives, and given to an alcoholic and a child molester. I knew I wasn't perfect, but I took care of them.

Losing my children like I had, pushed me to an all-time low. I constantly thought about committing suicide. I walked around in a fuzzy cloud. I constantly wrote letters to my children, apologizing for why I was going to take my life. I don't know how many times I wrote those goodbye letters either.

I spent many nights sitting in my bed contemplating how I was going to kill myself. I had pills for my back sitting next to my bed on the nightstand, along with a bottle of liquor. I wrote each of my children explaining to them that I loved them so much, and that I was sorry. I told them I wanted better for them. I apologized for us being separated. Instead of taking the pills, I would start screaming as I held my pet. As I screamed, it felt like someone had punched me in my belly.

My life was horrible. I was still dealing with my brother's stupidity. Things at work got harder and harder for me. Both fathers taunted me. They laughed in my face. They told me I never wanted my children. The alcoholic, and the child molester, had the nerves to tell me that their children were better off with them.

I called my kids like crazy in the beginning. They would tell me that they wanted to come home. Josh would allow me to sometimes see the boys on days that weren't mine. But then stopped because it wasn't my day. I couldn't believe them. I had never kept my children from them. Even if they wanted to see them on a day that was outside of their schedule, I allowed it. I always worked with them. I couldn't understand why they had become so hateful.

I now hated being at home. A house that had once been filled with laughter and joy was quiet. When I was at home, I sat on the floor crying for hours. I started to drink more and more. As if I had not been dealing with enough, I now received a 30-day eviction notice because my brother had been throwing parties when I wasn't home and cussing out neighbors. What else could go wrong?

On visitation days, I would give my children everything to make up for the time I wasn't with them. I literally spent my entire paycheck on things for them. I wanted to show them that I loved them. I wanted them to remember that they loved me. When they would leave to go back with their fathers, I went into a horrible depressive state.

I didn't know what to do without them. I continued to write suicide letters during that time. But never did it because I thought about the lies their fathers would tell them about me. So I fought to stay alive.

Now when I saw my children, I would tell them "mommy will fix it, remember I love you." After a while, my daughter started to hate me. She started to make up lies about me. She told her father that I was pulling her hair. She screamed when I came around. People asked me if I was beating her. I didn't know what was going on. But I knew she was angry. Not only did she not get to see me as much, she didn't get to see her brothers as much either.

I started to think that leaving my children would probably be the best thing for them. I thought that they would be happier. But then I remembered how it was for me not growing up with my biological mother. I thought about the hurt and the pain, and decided to abandon the thought of leaving them behind.

Everyone in town heard about what had happened to me. The women at my job laughed at me. I started to lie to people because I was so embarrassed. I didn't feel the need to explain my life situation to everyone.

The first year without my children was the hardest. I can still feel the pain at times. I will never forget it.

It was during that time that I grabbed my daughter, put her in the car, and hugged her. I told her how sorry I was that I couldn't be around, but I was still her mommy. I still loved her. She broke down and told me that her father had told her to not like me anymore. In response, I told her to remember all of our good times. I reminded her that she knew the truth deep down in her heart.

In that moment, I was so grateful that I did not take my life. I'm grateful that there had been something inside of me that kept me going. I know that it was only because of God that I am here because I felt dead inside during that time. But I was given strength every day to tell myself that one day my situation was going to be okay because my children would come back home.

As I waited for the day for my children to return home, I moved back into the house with my aunt and uncle. I was grateful for the change. I stopped going to the bars during this time. I drank at home because I was paranoid that if anyone saw me out, they would tell the judge that I was a bad mother, and I would get my kids taken away for good.

During this time, I had taken my daughter's father to court because of some of the things she had told me he was doing. Each time the judge ruled against me. He told me that what was reported was hearsay because I wasn't there. Even when Greg admitted to the judge that he had a problem with drinking, the judge found in his favor. He sent him to AA and gave him a pat on the back for admitting that he was an alcoholic and needed help.

It has been four years since my children were taken away from me. Although I haven't gotten them back through the courts, things were turning in my favor every day.

CHAPTER 19: **HER**

The night that I met her, the first woman I was romantically involved with, I didn't want to go out. That night I had an attitude for some reason, and only wanted to stay home. I had a lot on my mind with the situations with my children, my brother, and the new job I was about to start. And I thought that it would be boring.

Despite how I felt, my friends drug me out of the house anyway. When we got to the bar, I sat down instead of walking around dancing all over everybody. I didn't find it attractive being sloppy drunk anymore. So while all of my friends were out in the back, playing beer pong, I decided to hang back. I didn't want to be around smoke because I didn't want to have to rewash my hair.

While sitting there, my sister came back inside and said, "you're not having fun." Without hesitation I told her that I was ready to go, so I was going to find a ride home. She told me I couldn't go because she had just met up with someone that she wanted to introduce me to. I was annoyed because I had no desire to go outside to meet, or entertain, anyone. I didn't want to go. But because she begged me to come out, and wouldn't let up, I finally gave in.

She instantly became excited, took me by the hand and walked me out of the back door. As soon as we stepped out, I heard someone say, "ooh wee, you come here." I was instantly ready to pop off. As I looked to the right, ready to confront the person, I noticed a light skinned tattooed super fine man. My sister must have known by the way I stopped that I thought he was attractive, because she started laughing. I let her hand go and walked my little self right over there to him.

I looked him up and down. I was impressed. As I talked with him, I noticed a few things. He smelled good, dressed nice, was funny, and outgoing. As I peered into his eyes, I asked myself, "who is he?" And, "why haven't I seen him before?"

He must have liked what he saw too because we became very touchy-feely really quick. As soon as I walked over to him, he put his arm right around my waist. I liked that. It showed that he was really confident. After that, he didn't skip a beat. As we walked inside of the bar to get a drink, his hands slid down my dress and grabbed my butt. I couldn't believe it! Before I could say anything, we started kissing. Suddenly, the night had just gotten a whole lot better.

There had been something different about this man. I couldn't put my finger on it. Whatever it was, I knew that I liked it. After kissing, we danced and laughed, until it was time for me to go. But before I left, he asked me if I wanted to go on a date the next day, so we could really talk and get to know each other. Of course, I said yes. I enjoyed his company and I knew he enjoyed mine.

After taking him up on his offer, I leaned in and held the back of his head and gave him a hug, and got one of the biggest surprises of my life. Without saying anything, I stepped back, looked him in his face, and poked his chest. I asked him "what are those." In a very cocky way, SHE said, "boobs! They're nice, do you want to see them." I was shocked. I took another step back and said, "I'm not a lesbian. I don't like girls."

In that moment, so many different things were running through my mind. I had really been attracted to this girl. I couldn't believe it either. She looked like a whole man. She was tall and muscular, even had on boxers. Instead of getting upset with my reaction, she said, "you already promised me a date. You had fun all night, didn't you?" I said "yes, but I didn't know you were a girl." Her only reply was, "I'll see you tomorrow."

I couldn't believe what all happened that night. I went home, and I just kind of laid there, and thought about how much fun I had. I was stepping into new territory. I knew she was military, and only here for a couple of weeks. I had worked so hard to stay away from all of that. I didn't want to keep getting my heart broken over and over again.

I had so much going on the next day, but I decided to meet up with her to still hang out with her. Yes, I had originally thought it would be a bad idea. But after talking to one of my friends, who had dated a girl, I decided to take her advice and "try it" for myself. So I got the courage to text her. From there, we made plans to meet up at the bowling alley.

That night, I got all dressed up. I couldn't understand why either. I wasn't attracted to girls.

When I arrived at the bowling alley that night, I was greeted by her and her roommate. Even though we had made plans for it to be just the two of us, I didn't mind at all. The roommate being there was a little distracting because the attention and focus was more on her than anything else. But I still had a good time talking and laughing with them.

I noticed that different men looked her over. They were confused because they couldn't figure out whether she was a man or a woman. She looked like a woman, but she was very masculine at the same time.

I was very intrigued by this woman. She knew that I wasn't used to being with a woman, so she told me that we didn't have to rush into anything. She encouraged me to take things slow. She wanted to get to know me.

After that night, we started texting and talking like crazy. I thought about her all day long too. I kept asking her, "am I a lesbian?" She would always say "no, silly, you like who you like. You don't have to label yourself."

I started hanging out with her every day. She was extremely sweet and kind towards me. We did romantic things like laying under the stars. She would hold me and play with my hair as my head rested on her chest. She did this as she told me, "you have taken care of everybody else your whole life, just lay here and let me take care of you." She did, and said things that men had never said to me. Because of this, I started to feel happy again.

She was so genuine. She made me feel safe. She made me feel protected. For the first time in my life, I didn't care about having sex. For once, it wasn't about that. There was no feeling of being abandoned if I didn't do it either.

As time went by, we became more touchy-feely and flirtatious. We started to kiss with more passion. Things were heating up and we both knew it. So we finally talked about going forward sexually. I was scared. I didn't know what to do, or how to have sex with a woman. She was so patient with me. Without being too graphic, she explained to me that women can go buy their "parts," and take them off, and put them back into the drawer when they were done using them. I was dumbfounded but said, "okay."

When I finally had sex with her, it was different. There was no scratchy man face against mine, or his smell. For some reason, this made me feel more alive. To my surprise, I liked it. It didn't remind me of anything that I went through in the past. I didn't have to be drunk to have sex with her. For the first time in my life, I felt more free.

Before that moment, I never thought that I could have feelings for a woman. I never thought that I would be so comfortable either. I started to let the public know that I was with a woman by doing things like posting a meme on Facebook that said, "he is a she and I love it." I was now loud and proud. Nobody could take that feeling away from me either.

For the first time in my life, I was genuinely happy. I was determined not to lose her either. When she had to go back home, which was a couple of states away, I was determined to make it work. We spent many nights on the phone. At first, it was working. But the feeling of her not having me there was too hard. So hard that she tried to break up with me. I was not having it. I told her that she couldn't because it was my birthday. I knew that I had to do something, so I planned a surprise trip to visit her before her deployment.

When the date of the trip came, I was ecstatic. Because she had no clue that I was coming, I had to avoid her calls and make an excuse that I had to work. Everything started out well, but then quickly turned when my plane was delayed for a couple of hours. As I waited to board the plane, she called and texted me. I could tell that she was becoming more and more agitated because I wasn't responding. I ignored her calls because I didn't want her to hear the intercom and figure out what I was doing.

I was so relieved when I finally made it to her. As soon as she saw me her agitation left. I was so happy to be back in her arms. I missed her hugs so much. I missed just being in her presence. I soaked up every second I had, just lying in her arms. It was perfect.

Unfortunately, something shifted as my trip came to an end. I felt a disconnection in my heart. For some reason, I felt that it would be the last time that I was going to see her. The truth was that I couldn't give her the time that she wanted and needed. Even though she was trying to get stationed in a state that was closer to me, I still couldn't be with her. There was no way that I would be able to leave my children.

I was torn. I wanted her in my life. She made me happy. She made me feel alive. I couldn't go back to being unhappy.

When she left for deployment, we tried to maintain our relationship but couldn't. We talked a few times back and forth. But things became too much, so we ended things. I remember crying to her, telling her I was a lesbian and had no desire to be with a man again in life. She laughed and told me that other women were going to have a hard time dealing with me. She told me that because she was a different type of woman, was more masculine, that she could deal with me being a little rough around the edges. She encouraged me to focus on me and my children.

Instead of arguing with her like I had done with men in my past when I was unhappy with something, I cried. I wasn't mad at her for the decision she made. I was heartbroken.

After the breakup, I still didn't want anything to do with men. When they approached me, I would tell them that I was a lesbian. They always replied, "I'm going to turn you back straight." I laughed because I knew that they weren't. I was content with being with women.

CHAPTER 20: BECOMING LALA

With another failed relationship under my belt, I started looking for love on dating sites. I wasn't comfortable being single and alone. I was ecstatic when I connected with a woman who had been a music producer living in Las Vegas.

Even though I had been talking to other women online from Las Vegas, this one stuck out to me. It wasn't because of her looks either. It was because of her posts. She posted pictures in a mansion with Versace, Gucci and Fendi clothing. She was always standing by expensive cars, holding up stacks of money. She was always on the road with famous people. I just knew that she was rich.

During this time, I was working two jobs to save enough money to get a lawyer to represent me in my custody battle. No matter how much I worked, I couldn't save because I was spending so much money on my children. So when I saw her posts, I made it up in my mind that she could help me get money.

I was determined to get her attention. I posted all the best pictures of myself. Afterwards, I sent her a message in her inbox and waited. It took her awhile to finally respond back to me. When she did, she wanted to Facetime to make sure that I wasn't a catfish.

As we Facetimed, I noticed how unattractive she was. To continue talking to her, I had to keep thinking that she was going to help me. After the first conversation, we began to message and talk to each other quite often, even though she was always on the road with a bunch of different guys. And for an extended period of time.

When she got back home, the conversations between us changed. She started to tell me how beautiful I was. She told me how I could make money in a different way. She came right out and asked me if I had ever thought about being a stripper. Of course, I had not! I told her that I was a little too fat. Even though I was not big at this point, I thought that strippers had amazing bodies.

This woman wasn't fazed by my insecurities. She told me to send her pictures of my body. Which I gladly did. I was nervous about how she would respond. I was relieved when she told me that I only had a little bit of work to do. She always encouraged me by telling me to get on it.

Without skipping a beat, I started to work on my appearance. I started bleaching my skin because I thought that men were attracted to lighter skin. I started starving myself by going on different diets too.

I had my mind set on doing what I could to get to Las Vegas to become a stripper. I knew that I could dance. I had nothing to lose at this point. Everything I loved was already gone.

After getting my last two paychecks, I quit one of the jobs, and put in a leave of absence for the other. I had to keep it just in case I needed it to fall back on. That job had been a safety net for me. I had already been there for years. I'd be stupid to just let it go so easily.

With paycheck in hand, I put all of my stuff in my car and drove to Las Vegas. I was excited. I was really doing it. I was taking a big step towards getting the money I needed to get a lawyer, so that I could fight to get my kids back.

Several hours later, I pulled up to a beautiful high-rise behind the Wynn hotel. She was waiting on me. She quickly helped me take the trash and duffle bags with all of my clothing up to her place. Once inside, I peered at the beautiful view and ginormous shower, before she placed some diamonds around my neck. She did this before telling me how much she hated all my clothes.

The next day, she took me on a shopping spree to get a new wardrobe. She even made me an appointment to get my hair done in a weave. I was now set.

After the first week of being there, the time had come for me to prepare for my new career. We started to workout. I took a couple of pole dancing classes. I quickly learned that dancing and pole dancing were two different things. Through trial and error, I learned that it took great strength to pole dance. Strength that I did not have. I felt like a fish out of water as I flopped around that pole getting burn marks on my thighs and bruises on my feet.

I quickly learned that she had no sympathy for me. She treated everything like a business. I quickly started to feel like her employee. I wasn't even allowed to ask her questions either.

She requested that I wear makeup every day, even if I were in the house. I wasn't going to argue with her. I did exactly what she wanted. I had to do what was necessary. I had a plan and couldn't mess it up.

In the midst of my transition, I noticed how she seemed to be popular everywhere that we went. A lot of places we went, people would yell out her name. Some people would be surprised that they even saw her. I didn't understand what the big fuss was about until I found out that she used to be a famous pimp.

I had known early on that she had done time in prison; I assumed that it had been for drugs. But I learned that it was actually for pimping. But that wasn't the worst part. She had lied about her age to me, and was in prison with my biological mother.

Piecing things together, I now knew what she meant when she said I looked like my mom when she saw me. Even though she lied, I didn't care. I was determined to make money. She was willing to work with the fact that I couldn't miss my visitations with my children, so I was willing to work with her lying.

When my mother found out who I was in Las Vegas with, she lost her mind. My mom told me that she was a very dangerous woman.

I didn't care. I told her that she wasn't my pimp, she was my friend. My mom told me I had no clue what I was getting myself into.

Apparently, she and my mom both disliked each other equally. She told me that I couldn't hang out with my mom. She also wasn't allowed to come over to her house. She said my mom was ghetto and ratchet. She didn't want to be arguing and fighting with her.

As all of this was going on, I kept telling myself that I was in control. There was a purpose behind what I was doing. I reminded myself of how it was killing me emotionally to be close to my kids, but not able to be with them. I was doing this because I wanted to, it was my choice.

The time had come for me to start to work. I was excited. She explained to me that whenever I got home from work that I had to put the money in a bag and put it in the drawer. I told her that I wasn't giving her any of my money. I became agitated with her. She told me that she didn't need my money, but I had to because she had spent so much money on me when I first got there. She threatened to kick me out if I didn't listen.

I had not even started working yet. But I saw where this was going. I told her that I wasn't one of her girls, even though I knew it didn't matter. I knew that I officially had a pimp. And even though my biological mother didn't approve, she took me shopping to get my dancing gear.

I was told to buy specific things by my pimp. I even was told to bring the receipt back, like I had been a little kid. When my mom realized this it made her sick. She didn't want to be a part of any of it. But who else besides her was going to help me learn all that I needed to know? My mom was known for being one of the best strippers back in the day. I needed to learn her ways.

As we went from place to place, and appointment to appointment, my mom gave me some good advice. She told me not to link up with another black stripper because black strippers are actually more judged. She told me to play off of my Puerto Rican side. She told me to never dance just to one song, but to dance my butt off.

She reminded me that nobody in there was my friend. She schooled me about which colors to wear that would make me standout more.

By the end of the time I had spent shopping and talking to my mom, I was ready. I had all my gear in a stripper bag. Now all I had to do was get a place to hire me. That day, I called around asking whether they had openings. I had no idea that it took as much work as it did to get into a club. When I went to auditions, there were certain doors I had to walk through. I was in dressing rooms with 30-40 women sometimes. Those who were in charge of hiring looked at your face and body up and down.

It was humiliating. The bouncer would call your name. I had to walk up and down a red carpet, endure being ogled at, and called fat when I only weighed 145 pounds at the time. I never felt so ugly in my life. But I couldn't stop. After being rejected at three places, I finally got a yes.

I had to quickly learn all of the rules. You couldn't wear glitter or lipstick that was bright. Some clubs you could show your nipples, while you couldn't at others. Some clubs you had to make sure to keep your legs on the ground at all times, and couldn't just sit in a man's lap, but you could sit on the edge of the chair. Anyone who failed to follow the rules risked getting arrested for solicitation for prostitution.

I learned things very quickly. I did this by watching the other women. You would have thought that I really knew what I was doing on my first night. When it was my turn, I got up there, walked around the pole slow, shook my butt, and took my top off during the second song.

When a customer came in, I went right over to him and sat on his lap. All he wanted to do was talk. So I pretended like I was interested. As he asked me questions about myself, I quickly made up some garbage answers; I told him my name was LALA, and danced. That night, I made $200 off of him. I was happy, and so was my pimp.

When I got back home, she took my wallet and counted the money. Afterwards, she told me to put it in the drawer. I had forgotten about her rule that quickly.

With practice, I found my way. I sat on the laps of creepy men telling them whatever they wanted to hear, as they touched my body. I learned about stage presence, working the room, and how to climb all the way up the pole. I mastered running and falling down in split position. I became so good at what I did that I started to make $1,000 a night.

Every night, I came up and I put my money in the drawer. I only spent what was necessary for my hair, nails, eyelashes, and clothing. But I started to notice that money was missing. When I mentioned it to my pimp, she said that she didn't need my money. She claimed I spent it on upkeep. I let it go.

My pimp started to get verbally abusive towards me. She would start screaming about me. She told me that I needed to make more money because she wanted a Bentley. By that point, I was exhausted and knew that I needed to get out of there. But I needed to make as much money as I could.

When other strippers started selling themselves right out of the strip club, I initially wasn't on board with it. By then, I was already making a couple of hundred dollars more, which I now hid in my secret stash. So when they asked me to join them, I always said no. I didn't want to stoop down that low again. But when the opportunity presented itself again, I couldn't resist it.

That night, this man was giving me money left and right. When he offered me $600 to meet up with him in a hotel room, I thought, "why not?" That night, I left my car parked in the strip club parking lot, caught a ride to the hotel in an Uber, handled my business, and then went back to the club.

After that night, I started doing more than just stripping for men. I let guys bite my nipples. I rubbed their genitals a little bit more than I used to. I was willing to do anything for a couple of extra dollars.

During this time, I was catching the bus back and forth to see my children. Now, with the extra cash, I was buying them more toys and clothing. I think my aunt and uncle knew that I wasn't doing right. I was losing weight, and now wore weaves, and big eyelashes, along with long nails. In an attempt to stop me from going back to Las Vegas, they took my driver's license, so that I couldn't board the plane one time. Luckily, their plan did not work.

I had been so determined to get back to work after that trip. It was close to Christmas, and I needed to make more money to make it an extra special Christmas. The boys' father had agreed to allow them to stay with me in Las Vegas for two weeks. I was excited that they would be coming with me.

You would have thought that I would have taken a vacation during the time that they were there with me. But I didn't. I actually worked several times harder to make extra money for them. I wanted to provide them with an experience that they would never forget.

During this time, I took them shopping. I made sure that we did a lot of fun things during the day. I bought them a lot of gifts too. They had an amazing time. That is all that mattered to me. I wasn't even concerned about my wellbeing during that time. I was so tired from working long nights. My feet were sore. And I wasn't getting enough sleep because I had to create these great memories with them.

I would literally work all night until the early morning, come home just in time to make them breakfast, and I would get into bed to get a little sleep. I had my routine down.

One morning, after completing my morning routine with my boys, I got into bed and fell asleep as usual. While sleeping, I suddenly felt hands around my neck. I opened my eyes to see my pimp sitting on my back. She was choking me from behind. I was so confused. I started to cry as I clawed the bed begging for her to get off of me. She didn't listen. She started choking me even harder. I was beginning to lose consciousness. When I opened my eyes again, I saw my two little boys standing in the doorway watching. I yelled for them to run, but they wouldn't move. They stood screaming and crying. I started to tell her that she was killing me in front of my children. I begged her to please stop.

I couldn't understand why she was attacking me. I was making more money. I was coming home when I was supposed to. I didn't do anything to deserve this. I thought that I was really going to die in front of my children. Surprisingly, she got off of me. When I looked in her eyes, I could tell that she had lost her mind. She didn't even look the same.

I was unable to call anyone because she took my phone away from me. As I now lay on the floor begging for her to stop calling me names and taunting me, but she continued. She accused me of talking to my ex. I was confused because I wasn't. My boys continued to stay in the doorway crying and telling her, "my mommy is sorry." My pimp looked them in their eyes and told them that I was a bad mom. That I sucked d*** for a living. Hearing her say those things caused me to gain strength.

I jumped up from the floor and grabbed my children. I pleaded for her to leave my children alone. They were innocent and had nothing to do with anything. This agitated her even more. She got closer to me. Spit in my face and pushed me. I grabbed my boys and threw them into the shower with me. I started pounding on the bathroom walls to get the attention of the neighbors. I pounded on that wall for about an hour while she continued to scream. No one came to help me.

At some point, I got out of the bathroom and grabbed everything I could. My body was so sore. I don't even know where I got the strength to frantically run through the high-rise that morning, but I did. After I grabbed all the money from the drawer, I put it into a shoe box and gave it to my son to hold. I told him to not let it go.

She had finally given me my phone back. I wasted no time calling my mom. As soon as my mother heard my voice, she knew that something was wrong. All I could do was cry and beg her to come and get me. My mother became enraged. She screamed on the other end of the phone, "what did she do to you? I'm going to kill her." I didn't have time to explain everything, I told her I just needed to get out of there.

It took my mom a while to get to me because I didn't know the exact address. The pimp wasn't helping me give it to her. It seemed like she was scared of my mom. As I directed my mom to us by telling her the cross streets, the pimp kept screaming that she wasn't allowed to come up, or into the building. I didn't care what she was talking about. I just wanted to get out of there.

I was relieved when my mom finally got to us. We grabbed as much as we could and got in the car. Once inside, I broke down. I was an emotional wreck. I had bruises on my arms and my back. My entire back hurt. But I was grateful that I was finally safe.

That night, as I put my son to bed, I realized I didn't have his medicine. I asked him where the shoe box and everything was. He told me that he had sat them down when he was scared. I couldn't believe it. All of the money, thousands of dollars, was gone. That meant that I was broke. I had no idea what I was going to do to survive. But I couldn't worry about that. I had to get my son's medicine.

I had to message the pimp. I pleaded with her. I needed his medicine. Without it, he would get very sick. After a long time, and some convincing, she finally agreed to let me get it. But still stood her ground that my mom couldn't come in. I was fine with that. I wouldn't be asleep when I faced her this time. My kids were safe.

As I got ready to go get my son's medicine, rage took over me. I pulled my hair back in a ponytail. I put my shoes on. It was time for war. When I got to the high rise, the door man let me up. She let me inside when I reached her door. I looked at her and walked in. Once inside, I backhanded her. I told her to fight me now that my kids weren't there.

I snapped. Now I was the one spitting and screaming in her face. I pushed and hit her as she crawled away from me. She begged me to calm down. I snapped and started kicking the doors to the kitchen cabinets. I ran up the stairs and grabbed all of her expensive things from the closet. I grabbed them, along with a bottle of bleach. I then poured the bleach, and whatever other cleaners I could get my hands on, onto the gigantic grey leather sofas. I threw the bleach on the walls and whatever else I felt like destroying.

I destroyed everything while taking breaks in between to hit her. I screamed and cursed the entire time. I yelled for my money and my son's medicine. I eventually grabbed the shoe box and medicine, but not before I smacked her a few more times and spit in her face. Suddenly, she said she had enough and stood up as if she was ready to box. I was done. I had gotten what I needed.

When I got to my mom's house, I was shocked to find that there were only a couple of hundred dollars left in the box. This meant that I had to go back to work. I had to get my kids back home soon. Besides, I had to get out of my mom's apartment. I couldn't deal with the roaches that came out every time I cooked. I wasn't used to sleeping in a roach infested environment. Nor was I used to sleeping on a blanketed floor.

I was desperate. When the pimp messaged me, I played on her emotions. I told her what was going on. I told her about the roach infestation, and that I didn't have a bed. She caved and bought us new blankets, a really big air mattress, and some groceries. When my mom saw this it bothered her. She felt that I felt I was too good for this. I didn't care about what she had to say. It was all for my boys.

Their final days before taking them back to their father, I made sure that they had fun. I took them to buy clothes, get haircuts, and to go see the mermaids, and the aquarium. I had hoped that this would block the memory of them seeing me getting choked. I didn't want them to tell their father about that either. I wanted them to only talk about the good times they had with me.

While taking the boys back home, I stopped to see my daughter. Despite the fact that I bought her gifts, she wasn't interested. She was upset with me because her father lied and said that I didn't want her to go to Las Vegas. I was so annoyed with him when she told me this. He was the one who didn't want her to go. When I left her that day, she didn't seem like she cared. It hurt me so bad, but there was nothing I could do about it. I had to return to work.

Once I returned to Vegas, I moved back in with my pimp. As stupid as it was, I had to. I couldn't live in poverty. I wanted the money and the lifestyle I had with her. Now that I was back, she monitored me closely. She was constantly calling, screaming at me when she was there because she wanted me to make more money. I was fed up with her. When she came and watched me dance, I left the money she threw at me on the stage. This must have angered her because she started taking out money and throwing it on the other girls in the club.

I was more miserable now than I had ever been. But I needed to make money, so that I could save up to get the lawyer to get my kids back. In the midst of it all, I got a phone call from the supervisor of the job that I had been on leave from. I was told that I had been gone for too long. If I didn't go to work, I would lose the job for good. I knew that I had a decision to make.

After I found out that there was a possibility that my ex-girlfriend would be returning, I knew I had to get home. I had to be there just in case she really came back. I wanted and needed to feel the safety she brought. I decided to tell my pimp that I had to go back home for 9 weeks. I lied and told her that I would come back. She didn't believe me. To make her believe me, I left some of my stuff behind.

As I prepared to leave, I went to the money drawer and started taking money out. My pimp started screaming at me. She said I didn't need to take anything more than a couple of hundred dollars. I was going to be working there. I reminded her that my son's birthday was coming up. I needed money to throw a party. Seeing how she was acting, made me happy that I had hid money from her. If it had been left up to her, I would have left with little to nothing.

With some money from the drawer in hand, and the money I had been hiding, I boarded the bus for my final trip back home. I knew in my heart I would never return to my pimp no matter what. As I sat on that bus, I felt a sense of relief. I didn't care that I was now on a long bus ride home either. I was happy to finally be going home.

When my pimp realized that I wasn't coming back, she called and threatened me a couple of times. By this point, I didn't care. Before hanging up on her, I told her to give my stuff to my mom. I knew in that moment that I had lost everything. I was home for good.

CHAPTER 21: **HOME SWEET HOME**

When I moved back home, I returned to my uncle and aunt's house. I also returned back to my military job cleaning toilets. As much as I had known that it would be an adjustment, I really wasn't as prepared as I thought I was. No longer was I averaging $200 - $1,500 a day as I had been when I was stripping. I was only making $600.00 every two weeks. I couldn't stand working a normal job.

But I knew I had to stay there. There was absolutely no way I could return to stripping. Besides, my ex-girlfriend was on her way home to me.

The day she returned, my heart became excited. I couldn't believe that she was here. As soon as I saw her, I got out of my car and moved towards her. When I was close enough, she picked me up and I wrapped my legs around her. She held me like she was never going to let me go. I could feel the love and passion she had for me by the way she squeezed me. I finally felt safe again.

Being back with her was amazing. She didn't know what I had been through, so she didn't understand how much something as simple as a hug meant to me. With her, I was okay with living the simple life again. I preferred the small bedroom with a plastic sliding door, over the high rise, because it was with her.

I was completely at peace for the entire nine weeks we were together. Before that visit, I had never spent that much time with her. I enjoyed every minute of it, even though we didn't do anything besides enjoy each other's company. I loved rubbing her bald head as we laid in bed. I soaked up every minute of it!

Unfortunately, after she left for a long deployment, we broke up again. This left me feeling more heartbroken. I felt like nobody could love me through my situation. All they would ever see was a mess of a woman, who could never get it together. I was tired. I was drained. I felt like giving up.

But I couldn't give up. I never wanted my kids to see me as a failure. I never wanted them to feel like I just walked away from them. Because I felt this way, I went back to church. My mentor, who is a prophet, told me that I was his assignment. I broke down and cried when I heard this. I had never stayed in church for long. I was always in and out. But when I came back, people were always there for me, it still never seemed like enough though.

To feel the void that I now felt being home, I started to go on dating sites. I started talking to any woman who would speak to me. I needed the escape because everything in my life was getting hard for me. My uncle became controlling and a little creepy. He started making inappropriate comments towards me. So I started staying the night at other people's houses. I was literally couch surfing now.

I was grateful for the friends that I had. They let me stay at their place and use their car. This lasted for a period of 6 months. During that time, I only stayed at my house when I had to. I just couldn't take my uncle and his controlling ways. He tried to tell me what type of makeup to wear, requested that I cook dinner and serve him, as well as other things. I was disgusted because I had known him since I was 11 or 12 years old. When he told me that I didn't have to work because he would take care of me, I stopped talking to him altogether.

The more that things felt weird and out of control at home, the more I talked to people on the dating site. I ended up meeting someone that I could be open, raw, and honest with. When I told her that my life was a mess, she continued to talk to me. Suddenly. I started to find happiness with her.

The truth is that I could never be alone. I felt like I wasn't worth anything if I was by myself. I needed somebody else to want and love me because I didn't know how to love myself.

She, like my ex, was in the military. But she only lived five hours away. We talked all the time about everything and nothing. When she expressed that she wanted to come down and visit, I allowed her to. I let this complete stranger come into my home.

That night, I cooked a whole meal for her. It was pretty awkward as we sat at the dinner table with my aunt and uncle. They grilled her by asking her a lot of questions. And I sat there thinking about the fact that she was shorter than I had thought. She was also a little chubby. I wasn't used to this at all. My last two girlfriends were taller than me and they were buff.

Despite the fact that I wasn't that attracted to her, I continued seeing her. She drove down, either every weekend, or every other weekend. She did everything for me too. I was there for her at times. But I didn't treat her right. I was still bitter and hurt. Oftentimes, I took my anger out on her. Honestly, I never gave her a fair chance. If I didn't want to answer my phone for her, I didn't. If I didn't feel like talking to her for a couple of days, I didn't.

As I was doing these things to her, I didn't feel bad. I didn't care about her feelings. I treated her like things were her fault. I told her in the beginning that this was how I was. I had become heartless towards her.

No matter how bad I treated her, she still came down to visit me. She spent time hanging with my kids too. It made me feel like I had a family again.

I was really living a dysfunctional life at this point. I was in a dysfunctional relationship. I would tell her that she was not man enough for me. I knew this was silly because she was a woman. It didn't matter how much she dressed like a man, or shaved her head bald, or wore boxers, she was still female. It was hard to be with her because I felt like I was stronger and more dominant than she was. I felt like I could push her around, and I hated it. Even though

I hated everything about being with her, I stayed because I didn't want to be alone.

When I found out that she had a cocaine habit, I stayed with her. I remember it had been my 30th birthday. My plans I had made with my friends to party at a gay bar in California fell through when they didn't show up. Our dinner reservations also fell through. So her friends came over and we all started to drink. That's when the coke came out. People were asking me if I wanted to do lines. Of course not. I started throwing the drinks back instead.

We went to a small bar. After we arrived, people started coming in. The music that was being played was good. I watched her as she flirted with another girl. Instead of getting mad, I started dancing on the dance floor. She walked up and grabbed my arm. This set me off. It sent me into fight or flight mode. I was not going to allow anyone to push or hurt me again.

I started swinging on her. I fought her like I had no clue who she was. I lost my mind in that moment. When her friend tried to calm me down, I spit in his face and slapped him. I couldn't control myself. When she got in her car to drive away, I jumped in the backseat and started to swing on her.

We both got out of the car yelling and screaming at each other. She shoved me really hard. I fell over the curb and onto the ground. I heard my ankle pop. I instantly started crying as I held it. I called someone that I knew, who lived up the street, to come and pick me up. I was a drunk mess that night. I was literally five hours away from home fighting my girlfriend.

The next day, she came to pick me up to go to this paint and sip she had previously paid for. We talked as I made enchiladas like nothing happened. She rubbed my ankle, which was swollen and in a lot of pain. I couldn't bear to have any weight on it.

When I got home, I went to the doctor. I was told that I had some torn tendons. I had to wear a special cast on it. I didn't recover from the injury for months.

I knew that it had been my fault. I was embarrassed of my actions. I didn't talk to her for a while because of how things happened. She had apologized a thousand times to me. Eventually, I allowed her to come back around. She wanted to work things out.

I decided to not drink in front of her. I didn't want to get out of control anymore. I had never snapped so easily like that before. And I didn't want to snap like that again.

After we reunited, it was time for her to decide where she wanted to go. She was trying to get somewhere closer, like a different part of California. She understood that I couldn't leave because of my children, so she was trying to accommodate us. But it wasn't working. We argued a lot about it because I wanted her to do what was best for her career, while she wanted to do what was best for me.

CHAPTER 22:
NEW

With the status of my relationship being up in the air, I decided to branch out and get a new job. I had grown to hate my job cleaning rooms. I knew I needed something completely different. I needed to feel more validated.

I was paying so much in child support at the time, that it caused me to barely get by. So I took a leap of faith and applied for a factory job with 12-hour shifts. It paid $17.00 an hour, and offered overtime. I was hired the same day that I interviewed.

I loved my new job. Even though I was exhausted from getting up so early in the morning and returning late at night, it was so freeing. It was nice being around people who didn't know me. This meant that there wasn't any gossip about me because they didn't know my life.

I started to feel like I was exactly where I was supposed to be. My paychecks were bigger than I was used to receiving from a regular job. After working overtime, I was making $800-$900 per week. This meant that I would be able to get my own place soon.

Instead of being happy for me, my girlfriend was jealous. I was now making more money than she was. I couldn't understand why it was a problem either. I was now able to take care of myself and my children better. I felt like she should have been happy for me. Even though she wasn't, I didn't let her stop what was going on in my life.

I now had a job and schedule that afforded me the opportunity to be there for my children. I was able to make my work schedule around my boys' soccer schedule. I was already missing too much of their life at this point, so I refused to miss their soccer games. Soccer was important to them, so it was important to me. It was something that Danny could do freely without worrying about having a seizure.

Things were going well for me. I even met another lesbian who I quickly became close friends with. She and I had a lot in common. She had also been in the foster care system. Her mother, like my mother, also had been addicted to drugs. She was one of the sweetest souls, who sympathized with me instead of judging me.

Although she had been nothing but kind to me, I still didn't tell her the things that I had been through. I was ashamed. I didn't like the things that I had done. They were things that I wanted to keep secret. So I opted to lie about the situation with my kids and my financial status. I spoke about the life that I wanted to live. I literally started to live in this fantasy.

During our friendship, I started to stay at her house on the days that I worked. It was easier for me to drive back and forth to work from there. I would only go home when I had to get my children for visitations.

My section at work began to grow during this time. With that, I was growing too by picking up things pretty quickly. Because of it, my lead loved my work ethic, and wanted me to become a lead as well. I was excited about this. It meant that I would be making over $20.00 an hour if I were in that position. I knew that the opportunity would be good for me and my children, so I started to work even harder.

My plans to obtain the lead position were thwarted when my lead was promoted to another position. The supervisor that was put in his place brought 10 different employees with him. They were all new and needed to be trained by me. To my surprise, and without a valid reason, the new supervisor had no faith in me. He didn't allow me to rise to the occasion. This was hard for me. I wasn't used to it. My previous lead gave me full rein and encouraged me.

The new supervisor looked down upon me and other women. He was sexist. There was also some racism. He literally came and tore our section apart. Before he came, we were all close. We were like family. Now there was so much cattiness and racism.

Because of this change in environment, things became depressing for me all over again. When the time came for me to go up as lead, he told me to fall back. He discouraged me by telling me that I was never going to get that position. That I didn't know anything. He even made me stop training other people. This meant that I now was just another worker.

I filed complaints against him on different occasions. Other people in our section did as well. But nothing was ever done about what he had done or said. He literally spent our morning meetings cussing us all out as if it were okay. It got to the point that I dreaded going. This middle eastern man took his time to call us monkeys and sand niggers. He even body shamed this 300lb woman. He would purposely hit her with the boards and make her walk faster than she could. I really couldn't believe how much stuff he got away with.

When I decided that I wasn't going to be a part of the drama, or go along with what was being done, I was labeled. He accused me of not being a team player. I literally started coming to work and putting on my headphones. I stopped speaking to everybody.

I became more focused on doing my job. I clocked in and clocked out. I was no longer going over and beyond. I was there to get a paycheck and that was it.

My attitude started to show during this time. I would become fed up with him cussing us out all of the time. So I walked up to him a couple of times and let him know that I didn't appreciate the way that he talked to me. I was stressed; just because he was my boss, that didn't give him the right to be condescending. This made him hate me even more.

Now that I had this big target on my back, I waited for him to fire me. I loved my job, and didn't want to lose it because I was making good money. But he made things uncomfortable and hard for no reason.

During all of this, I was still dating my girlfriend. I told her a little of what was going on, but held back how I was getting myself into certain situations. I only told her what she needed to know because the dynamics of our relationship had changed. I lacked a lot of respect for her because it was now getting closer to the time for her to move down south.

I was mad about everything. I told her that if we didn't get married, we might as well break up. I said this because I thought if we got married that it would give us a better chance of staying together. And it would mean that we would be doing better financially with the added money. After tossing the idea of marriage around we decided to do it.

I decided I didn't want a big wedding. I only wanted to party with my closest friends. So we decided to rent an Airbnb in Las Vegas. I decided that my children wouldn't be there. I really didn't care about the ceremony or the vows. It was all about the alcohol, my outfit, and how much fun it would be for me. I really looked at it more as a vacation, not a wedding.

Before I went to Las Vegas for the wedding, I knew that it was something that we should not be doing. My girlfriend was a mess, while everyone was excited and partying. She sat alone doing nothing. She didn't even want to talk to anyone. We literally argued almost every single day that we were there.

After a while, her mood seemed to change. She started acting fun-loving again. Little did I know that this was only because she had gone into the bathroom and did some coke. I had no idea that the fun-loving person I had met and decided to marry was a result of the coke that she had done. She hid it so well.

Before we actually took our vows, I started to notice how she didn't want to walk next to me, or hold my hand. I told her that we didn't have to get married. We could just continue to party. We had already paid for everything beforehand, so it wasn't like we would be left with a bill or anything. She kept saying that that wasn't the issue, and that everything was fine. So we went ahead and got married.

On our wedding day, everyone looked so nice. I wore a beautiful maroon dress. She wore a nice suit. Instead of exchanging wedding rings, she gave me a necklace. My biological mom was the one to walk me down the aisle. Afterward, we went out to dinner at a Brazilian steakhouse.

That night, we went to the Airbnb instead of going out as planned. There I was, married a second time. But this time, instead of having a husband, I had a wife.

As soon as we returned home, everything was business from there on out. I had to get my military card so that I could have access to different things. She had to provide the proper paperwork to them so that she could get paid more. All so that we could qualify to get a home.

Because I was now married, my uncle insisted that I move out. He said that I was no longer his responsibility because I chose to marry somebody else. We were now stressed out because we had spent all of the money we had on the wedding.

I started to work more overtime to get the money we needed. My wife began getting different loans so that we would have as much money as we could when something popped up. There had been a long waitlist for houses in the area. We knew that we had to have everything in place. Time was not on our side.

As all of this was going on, I received a call from one of my mentors from church. He's not only a mighty man of God, but he is also related to the pastor. He told me to try to make it out to a revival that the church was having. I told him that my work schedule was busy, but I would try to make it out. This had been the first time that I had been personally invited to go to church. I was excited because

I loved when he preached. I had never seen somebody preach like him before. He was the first person that I had ever heard prophesy.

I was actually able to make it out to the revival service. I received a prophecy that night. I was told that I was going to have enough money to get my children back. I was told to not leave my position at work and to stand still. He looked at me several times and firmly said, "stand still."

I knew God had spoken through him. I was crushed and happy at the same time. Happy because I would be getting the money I needed for the lawyer to get my children back. But I was crushed because God wanted me to stand still at a job where I was being belittled and treated like garbage. I didn't understand it. I asked the prophet what he meant. He grabbed me and told me to stand still. His eyes had been wide open as he stared at me. I still didn't understand why; I hated to stand still in a position that I hated so much.

But those words stayed with me. I continued to question what they meant and why I had to. But I knew that I had to because God was moving that night. There had been too many holy things that had happened for me to deny it. I left there that night feeling a lightness I had never felt before. Something was different.

What I didn't know at the time was that my pastor was trying to save me. He had heard what I was going through. He had heard that I was going to get married to a woman (he didn't know I had already married her). He knew that I liked how his nephew preached and prophesied, so he sent him to reach out to me, so that I could get a breakthrough. That showed me just how much my pastor loved me. Even though I was in and out, and would not come that often, he never stopped caring.

After hearing what God had said, I tried to make it happen myself. I had been naive. I wasn't fully in church back then, so I started to think about different ways that I could get a big check. I started gambling thinking that that was the way to get it.

I did end up putting money in my pocket here and there. But I became addicted to gambling. I always thought that I was going to hit it big, so I gambled more and more. I continued down this path until I started to realize that I was losing a lot of money.

CHAPTER 23:
AGAIN

I heard about a house that had been for rent. Although the landlord was crazy and racist, I was determined to get it. It was a four-bedroom home with two bathrooms, two living rooms, and was located near a park. All I could think about was how perfect the home was for the kids. I had to have it and would not take no for an answer.

Although I had developed a gambling addiction, we still had the money we needed to secure the home. So after going back and forth with the owner, with him saying yes and saying no a few times, he finally allowed us to move in. I was ecstatic. I finally felt like I was getting somewhere again. I now had a house. I had a good job. And I finally had my wife.

My home quickly became the hangout spot. It was well kept and decorated. It was warm and welcoming. My friends, who were more like family, enjoyed coming over for dinner, holidays, and barbecues. My kids also enjoyed running around because there was so much room for everybody.

Although my wife stayed in San Diego, it still felt like we were a family. Because she traveled back and forth a lot to be with me, it felt like we were actually together. Her stuff was in the home, and her dog was there too.

Everything was working out between us until she relocated to the south. I had always been worried that if she went there, things between us wouldn't work out. I felt this way because she would be close to her hometown. I assumed that she would find somebody else.

My wife being back in the south, along with my insecurities, and her drug use, caused a wedge to be placed between us. A lot of animosity now came out. We started to behave like we were making transactions, not like we were married. It became just about money.

Things in the home became hard for me around the same time. I wasn't working as much overtime, so paying bills became a problem. The bills for this big house kept piling up on me. I knew we needed extra money, but I knew that there was no way that I could work an extra job. My wife working an extra job was out of the question. I knew that I needed to do something, such as working from home, to bring in extra income.

I started searching for any opportunity to make money. This led me back to an old habit. I found a job working as a phone sex operator. I thought this had to be easier than dancing. It wouldn't require people to touch me. So I enrolled in a course that taught me how to keep people on the phone. I learned that despite popular belief, I wasn't selling sex, I was selling minutes.

I quickly learned that the men on the other line were extremely concerned with whether or not they were talking to the girl in the picture. They would ask me a thousand different questions that made the job more tedious than any job I had ever known.

My wife knew everything that I was doing. She even helped me to find my portfolio. I had decided that I would be Tammie, a lonely middle-aged white woman whose husband was cheating on her. To my surprise, a lot of men liked her. On my days off, I spent the entire day on the phone listening to guys talk dirty. I played into every one of their sick fantasies. Whenever it became too real for me, I would hang up.

As uncomfortable as it was, the job working as a phone sex operator brought in the extra cash that I needed. As good as the money was, I was becoming mentally drained. I literally spent my entire day talking about sex.

At the end of the day, I saw it as just another job. It was a way for me to make money. Like with most jobs, this one became tiring too. It started to interfere with my relationship with my wife. I didn't even want to talk to her on the phone because I had become so concerned with missing out on making money.

Being with my wife started to seem pointless to me. We no longer agreed on anything. It started to feel like she wasn't trying to be a part of our lives anymore. So I started to do my own thing. I started dating more women who looked manlier than she did. This did something to me. I constantly kept feeling like I had the best of both worlds.

I now told my wife that whatever I did was my business, and whatever she did was hers. I didn't want to know what she had been doing out there in the south. I wanted her to keep it to herself.

I started to feel normal around this time. My daughter was coming around me more and more. The boys' father was also letting them come home too. I started to live my life like I used to.

I started going back to the bar every Friday night. I needed the drinks to relax. Work was extremely draining. It became more demanding. I hated it, and was always ready to walk out. But I stayed put because of God telling me to stand still.

I allowed my little brother to move in again even though I thought that it was a bad idea. I knew that he and I argued, and I didn't want certain things that he did around my children. But I went against what I was thinking because of him saying that he was trying to do better. He had just had a new baby, and wanted to do right this time. I couldn't turn my back on him, so I let him come.

Everything he said was a lie. Like before, I found myself constantly arguing with him about having people hanging out at my house. He had girls coming in and out. My front room now smelled like weed. I was so frustrated.

To make matters worse, my landlord hated him. Apparently, my brother had rented from him before and screwed him over. My landlord didn't want him there. He started to sit outside of my house, watching to see if my brother lived there. I told my brother that I didn't want to be kicked out of my house because of him. But he didn't care.

CHAPTER 24:
NOVEMBER 27th

I went to work like every other day. That day, I was doing quality inspection, which was my favorite task at work. There was a new kid in front of me who needed a little bit of help, so I pushed some parts to the next table. All of a sudden, they started falling off the table. Instantly, I thought, "oh, my goodness this part cannot fall on the ground. That's thousands of dollars wasted." The front part of the pile was stuck, and the other tiles started to break. I stretched out my hand and the parts fell into my hand. I used all my strength to push them back on the table. Some of them hooked to my shirt and pulled my shirt. I wasn't worried about my shirt though; I kept thinking "thank goodness these parts didn't fall ."

I was so frustrated with those stupid tables. There had been so many other people who have had the same issue. After saving the parts from falling on the ground, I went to pick something up and noticed my hand didn't move. I couldn't grab anything. I wasn't in pain or anything, but my hand was a little sore. I felt a pinch, so I taped my wrists thinking that it would be okay.

My supervisor asked if I was okay. I said "yes," because at that moment I thought I was. I tried to pick something else up, and I still couldn't move anything. I had no feeling. It was like I was telling my hand to do something and there was no connection between it and my brain. The kid's eyes, who was in front of me, got big when he saw this. I let my supervisor know that there was a definite problem. I went downstairs to the medic. The medic then directed me to a nearby clinic because my injury involved my wrist.

My supervisor, who I couldn't stand, had to drive me to the clinic. As we walked to his car, the pain started to set in. After waiting at the clinic for about 2 hours, they decided to do an x-ray. The x-ray tech told me, "well, I'm not supposed to tell you anything, but this right here, definitely isn't right." I said, "what do you mean?" He just kept pointing to my x-ray as he said, "I can't tell you, but something isn't right."

Once the doctor reviewed my x-ray, and made a phone call to another doctor, I found out that my wrist had been dislocated in an odd way. I started crying because I had never had surgery. They gave me a pill, and then sent me to the ER. I was extremely scared. I called my wife immediately to let her know what was going on.

That morning the ER was packed. People were already telling me that they had been there for 3, 4, and 5 hours. I went to the ER at about 10 am, and didn't get out of there until about 5:45 pm. Once they called me to the back, they started doing more x-rays. The doctor was concerned about my arm and why it wasn't broken further up. They gave me morphine for pain. I called my wife and had her call my boss to tell him that I get delusional when given certain kinds of pain meds. Once the medicine kicked in, I started dying laughing because there was a bunny on the TV. I was so high, it was ridiculous. I kept apologizing to the doctors and laughing at the TV.

Before they discharged me, they put a temporary hard cast on me, and told me that I was going to have to see a bone specialist because they were worried about my ulnar nerve. But before I could see the bone specialist, I had to see a workman's compensation doctor to get the necessary approval. The workman's compensation doctor couldn't get me in for a couple of days.

In the meantime, I was off of work for 4 days. Those 4 days were gruesome. I screamed and cried because I had never been in that much pain in my life. I kept saying that I would rather give childbirth than to deal with the pain. I didn't know what was going on. It felt like there were pins and needles rushing through my body. Nobody understood why I was in so much pain for just a simple dislocation. I would wake up in the middle of the night screaming bloody murder. It felt like my whole right arm was on fire.

I couldn't do anything either. I was laying on my couch in pain wearing the same funky pajamas for days. The pills that I was given to manage the pain, weren't doing anything. I finally went and saw the workman's comp doctor. They cut my hard cast off like it was no big deal. Afterwards, they grabbed my wrist roughly. I kept saying ouch, and trying to pull my arm back to me. I had already done my research and knew that it was in my best interest to not allow them to push me around. Their only goal was to get you back to work.

After he was done grabbing my wrist, he told me that it wasn't dislocated. I told him that I was going to see a bone specialist. I then asked him how he knew that it was not dislocated if he hadn't done any x-rays himself. I informed him that I had a picture of the x-rays on my phone, and you could clearly see that it was dislocated. I also reminded him that three different doctors had already confirmed that it had in fact been dislocated.

I was not going to allow this doctor to send me back to work like everything was fine when it wasn't. I knew my body. I knew that something was terribly wrong.

I got an attitude with him when he decided he was going to try to put the cast that he had taken off back on. They all became annoyed with me when I told them to put the new cast on correctly. I was bothered though because he didn't refer me to the right doctor.

As a result of how the workman's compensation doctors treated me, I decided that I was going to need a lawyer. There were too many hoops that I had to go through to get the medical attention I needed. Everyone didn't believe you. It would take me two to three months to see the doctor I needed. I even had people following me back and forth to the doctor's appointments.

I became very angry. I was treated like a criminal when I was the victim. I had gotten hurt on the job. A job that I still had to show up for during this process. Yes, I had modified duty. But it still didn't ease the pain, or make my commute to work any easier.

To get to work, I had to leave my house at 2 am, when I didn't even have to be there until 6 am. This was all because I could only use my left hand to drive.

I now needed help to do simple tasks. I couldn't put my hair in a ponytail. I couldn't button my jeans. And I now needed help taking care of my family.

I was a little relieved when the bone specialist confirmed that my wrist was in fact dislocated. In fact, he said that he had only seen the type of dislocation I had three times in his career. He also said that I should have broken my whole arm. Because it had not broken, they were worried. Fifty pounds had fallen on my wrist without breaking my whole arm.

After doing an MRI, and seeing that things appeared okay, the doctor asked if I wanted to have surgery and pins put in my wrist. He told me that I would lose range of motion with the pins in my wrist. I started to cry because I never wanted surgery. I was scared of surgery. So I asked if there were other options. The doctor said that he could possibly roll it back into place right there in the office. He warned that it would be extremely painful, and he would have to put a hard cast on me for eight weeks.

I decided to go with the latter option. The day of the procedure, a friend came to the appointment with me. As part of the preparation, before the doctor came in to roll my wrist, they put some super cold stuff all over my arm. To my surprise, it hurt me. It made my arm feel numb, and like there was a sharp razor going deep down into it. I was already panicking, and the doctor hadn't even done anything. I was scared to say the least.

The next thing I knew, they were putting a big needle in my wrist. I was horrified because I am afraid of needles. Once he was deep enough, he released some more numbing medicine into my wrist.

I felt a burning sensation. I cried as I cussed up a storm. The doctor kept asking if I was sure I wanted to go through with the procedure. I told him yes. Next thing I knew, he grabbed my wrist and started talking to me. I told him that I knew what he was doing: trying to distract me.

Slowly, he rotated my wrist. I started to move my feet as I cussed. It hurt like hell, so I couldn't help but to arch my back and wiggle my toes like a child. Then with one big push, my wrist was pushed back into place. Afterwards, he put a cast on all the way up to my armpit. The doctor had faith that everything was going to work out just fine.

Everything was difficult to do with that cast. I couldn't even shower properly, so I decided to bathe instead. At night, I cried because of the deep pain I felt in my bone. No matter what I took, the pain would not subside. Everyone, including my brother, thought that I was faking the pain.

I was also under the influence of pills because of the pain. I literally would sit at work in a corner trying to operate a machine with tears running down my face. I honestly shouldn't have been working because I couldn't operate the machine that they had me on. I had to call a coworker every few minutes to help fix the machine because I couldn't do it.

I couldn't even eat my lunch at work because of my limited mobility. No one offered to help me either. I cried so much during that time.

It had been a couple of weeks after my wrist was reset, and the pain wasn't getting better. I knew that something was wrong. I went back to the doctor and told him that my arm felt like it was on fire, but it wasn't burning. I also described to him how I felt like someone was stabbing me. After listening to my concerns, he cut the cast off and sent me for x-rays. According to the x-rays, everything looked fine.

I felt crazy! The doctors started to give me more pills like Gabapentin and Lyrica. I was also given numbing gel. The pills just knocked me out. They did not take away the pain. While I was in deep sleep, my son had a seizure and I didn't even hear him. In the past, I always was able to hear him having a seizure because of the noise that was caused. My daughter and my baby son had to take care of him. I knew in that instant that I had to stop taking the pills they had given me.

The only problem was that I didn't know how to deal with the pain. My brother suggested that I smoke weed. I didn't like weed because it made me paranoid and act stupid. But I started to smoke weed a few times a day. It definitely took the pain away. But I got too dependent on it.

The time finally came for my cast to come off for good. I was excited. When they took it off, a shooting pain went up my arm. I grabbed my wrist and told the doctor that it was still broken. It looked at me like I was insane, but did another x-ray. The x-ray showed that everything was fine. The doctor told me that maybe everything was in my head. So he referred me to a physical therapist and another bone specialist to work on the carpal tunnel syndrome that I had received from the injury.

Once I started going to physical therapy, there was nothing that they could do for my hand. He directed me to move my fingers little by little. He asked me to try to pick up things like a grain of rice. It was difficult. I still had no range of motion in my wrist, and barely any feeling in my fingers.

When I saw the new bone doctor, he wanted to do surgery. But decided against it because he found a bigger problem. He sent me to a neurologist which took a couple of weeks. He then stated that I needed a special physical therapist who only dealt with hands.

As soon as I saw the neurologist, I was given an EMG test. It had been around that time that I was assigned a case manager by workman's comp. I was so worried. I knew that these case managers were not working for me. My lawyer told me that I didn't have to talk to the case manager.

The neurologist performed different tests on both of my arms. He was very concerned with my right arm. He thought that I was too young to be dealing with the issues that I had with it. He told me that I had a very rare disease called complex regional pain syndrome 2 (CRPS 2). He explained that it is something that lasts greater than 6 months, in which there is a disconnection in my nervous system. My nervous system was still telling my arm that it was broken. My nerves were in hyperdrive. This caused the slightest touch to feel heavier than it should. When my arm got too cold, it hurt, and when it was too hot, it was irritated.

The pain at times went from my spinal cord to my brain. According to the doctor, I had one of the most painful diseases. According to the McGill pain chart, it was ranked above everything, including pain associated with childbirth and phantom limb disorder.

When I would hit my arm even the slightest bit, it would spasm and shake. This left me with no control over it. When my fingers start to spasm, you can actually see the contraction. Oftentimes, I looked down at my hand watching it contract and spam with tears rolling down my face.

The doctor told me that it was very important for my hand to get desensitized. He even said that the burning and stabbing sensation was from the disease. I was happy that I had some kind of diagnosis, even though it wasn't the one I wanted. I knew that I was not crazy.

I found out that CRPS 2 was also termed something else. The suicide disease. So many people who had it could not take the pain because they were told that they were faking it, or doctors couldn't understand how to deal with it. My doctor encouraged me to not go home and do any research on the internet because I would be devastated.

I was very blessed from the beginning. I had a wonderful team of doctors. I believe that God purposely placed all of them in my life. My case manager for workman's comp even signed off on all my doctors' appointments, even though she was the only one against me.

That day, my doctor yelled at her as he told her that I should have already been seeing a hand specialist. He told her that I needed to see a pain psychologist and pain management doctor. He was furious that there had been so many months in between my doctor's appointments. He voiced his concern with her taking her sweet time when there is normally a six-month window when you can reverse things. I was coming up to that mark pretty quickly. I needed the hand specialist to start the process of desensitizing.

The process of desensitizing was painful, but I allowed it to happen. They put my hand in hot wax, a sand machine, beans, and rice. They rubbed and pulled my fingers a lot too, while I cried. They apologized the entire time. I knew that they were doing their job and it was for my greater good.

The doctor was always really concerned. He told me that there was no cure for this disease. I broke down crying like, "what do you mean no cure?" He told me that physical therapy was my only hope. I was devastated.

During this time, I was sitting at work. I sat in that chair and cried every day. I listened to Tasha Cobbs' album on repeat to help get me through the day. I sang "gracefully broken" and "break every chain," over and over again. There was something about her voice that helped me.

Before this point, I would only listen to podcasts; sexual podcasts, murder podcasts, and everything else. But, now, I deleted them off of my phone and would only listen to uplifting things.

With all of the pain medication that I was on, and the required doctor appointments, I was only allowed to work part-time. Everyone, including my new case manager, agreed that I was dealing with a lot, and was tired and groggy from the pain pills. From that point on, doctor appointments became my life. I was so relieved when they decided to put me on medical leave.

During one of my appointments, I became more hopeful when my new physical therapist that I was seeing three times a week, told me that I didn't have CRPS. I said okay. I was willing to believe anything, so if she said I didn't have it, that was good enough because I sure didn't want this disease. I wanted my arm back and I wanted to feel better. As she began to work with my hand, we saw a little progress. We both became excited.

CHAPTER 25: **TRANSITIONS**

My freedom was taken away from me when I became injured. I couldn't do my hair on my own. I had to wait patiently for others to tie my shoes. I often found myself upset at others because they didn't do things the way I liked. It was difficult for me getting used to this new norm.

It was during this time that I realized that my wife and I's marriage was over. She had only come down to see me once after I had gotten injured. During that visit, I still had on my cast. I took my anger out on her because she didn't come to see me. I was frustrated. I cried a lot about my new condition. I never thought that I was going to overcome it. I accepted that I wasn't going to be able to do anything in life. So I told my wife that I knew that we were not together anymore. I asked her to continue to pay the rent. I knew that she couldn't be there for me. Nobody knew how to deal with my situation.

I had started to experience more symptoms. My arm started to swell up, doubling in size, my fingers started to visibly twitch uncontrollably. I started to grow hair on my arm like a man. And I would sweat under my arms constantly to the point that I placed feminine pads in my t-shirt to soak it up.

During this time, I was very emotional. I had gained a lot of weight because of the different pain medications they had put me on. I found comfort in food. Eating kept me happy. I would sit and eat a whole pizza, chips, multiple sandwiches, without caring. I drowned my emotions in food.

I was depressed and jealous of those around me who were dating. There were men and women who wanted to date me, but I couldn't do it because I didn't know how I would be able to tell them about my arm.

I could no longer hide my feelings behind makeup or clothes. Now it showed. Someone only had to take one look at me to see it. I was miserable. I started to ask, why me? Why did my life have to be so hard? I didn't want to live anymore. I felt like I was constantly enduring.

My landlord decided that he wanted us out. He had found another family living in a van. He felt bad for them, so he wanted us out to move them in. I couldn't believe what I was hearing. We had always paid our rent on time, but he wanted us out. I begged him not to. I cried as I pleaded with him.

He had been fully aware of my situation with my arm and he wanted to just kick us out. My wife was not able to come and help me pack. I didn't know how I was going to pack up the house. Thankfully, I had family and friends that came over on different days to help me pack up the house.

While all of this was going on, I stopped making progress in physical therapy. My hand started to get worse. My therapist told me that I had the worst case of complex regional pain syndrome that she had ever seen. She apologized because she didn't know what to do. This broke my heart. I cried and told her that she had tried her best. It wasn't her fault that my hand would not desensitize.

Not knowing what to do, or where to go, I started going to church again. I was in church more than ever now. I literally soaked everything up, not just on Sundays, but on Wednesdays too. We were learning about our ear gates, eye gates, and prayer. During one of the services, I went up for prayer. I was told that I would be healed. At that time, I couldn't even hold a pencil in my hand because of the pain. Miraculously, I was able to pick up one of the flags that they had at the church. I started to wave it with my hurt hand. I even began to clap a little bit more too.

God told me to go through the process, but I had to do everything they asked me to do. He let me know that everything was going to be okay. I knew that I was going to be healed, even though I didn't know when. But until that time came, God kept showing me signs to confirm it. My finger wiggled, and my hand opened up one night during prayer.

With these signs from God, I started to realize that I serve an awesome God. I knew that life and death is in the power of the tongue, so I stopped speaking negativity. I started telling people, including my physical therapist, that I was going to be healed. I believe that God wanted to show people that healing is still real; that he can take away the worst pain, and give me full range of motion, all for His glory.

As I waited on my physical healing, God told me to go home to my adoptive parents. At that time, I had been sleeping on my friends' couches. I didn't understand why I had to go back there. I couldn't even get along with them. I refused. I wasn't going to do it because I was so angry and bitter about the things that had happened in my childhood. I hated going over there. Even though I lived in the same town as them, I didn't see them, and I was fine with that.

Instead of listening to God, I moved into a two-bedroom apartment with my brother. At the time, workman's compensation hadn't started to pay me anything yet. My wife wasn't paying my rent anymore. She'd only give me a couple hundred for groceries. Even though I was back sleeping in a room with my children again, I was grateful.

CHAPTER 26: BREAKING STRONGHOLDS

As I continued going to church, I decided that I wasn't going to drink anymore. My pastor had been teaching us about how fasting and prayer can break strongholds. At the time, I didn't even understand that drinking had been a stronghold. But after hearing his teaching, I wanted to start turning my life around.

Wednesday night bible study became prayer night. My pastor started to ask us to pray. At the time, I didn't even know how to pray. I didn't know how to be led by the Holy Spirit. But I started to pray what I wanted God to do for me. I prayed for healing for every child. I prayed for every single person in the church. This was how I prayed for quite some time.

My pastor told us that if we ask God to take something away, He could take the very taste of things out of our mouth. From that moment, I began to fast, and pray, "Lord, help me to not drink. I no longer want alcohol." During that time, I would drink occasionally. But when I went to my sister's house after I started to pray and fast, I filled our glasses to the top with wine. I took a sip, and sat the glass down. It didn't taste right. I was confused because it was the brand that we always bought. A couple of days later, my brother came over to my sister's house. We got a bottle of wine. I poured some in my cup, took a half sip, and didn't want it.

I couldn't even stand the taste of wine any longer. I was dumbfounded. The very taste for it was gone from my mouth. I had literally been drinking every day, but now I just stopped. I started to laugh. I really asked God to take the taste away from me and He did!

Church became more interesting. It was no longer something that I was forced to do. I wanted to go. I needed to go. I felt full when I went. I started to get a deeper understanding and knowledge of the word of God. Now everything that was said made sense.

I started to understand that there are such things as demonic spirits running rampant through the earth. This is the reason why people struggle and are bound to things like alcohol and sexual perversion. It wasn't just because somebody chose to be like that. They were actually bound. Before learning this, I never saw it like that. I never knew there was such a thing as a spirit of depression and anxiety.

I also started to understand about spirits called destiny assassins. These are actually things in the spirit realm that we could not see, but their assignment is to tear us down. Their assignment is to make sure that we do not complete our assignment. I learned this is all possible because Satan knew who we were and are meant to be, so he purposely leads us into all of this mess. He unleashes different distractions from different angles on us, so that we would stay bound. His entire goal is to keep us from completing God's work.

I realized all the warfare that I had gone through wasn't necessarily something that I had done wrong. It was because the enemy knew that God had a purpose for me, and that He wanted to use me. The devil put all these different distractions in the form of different relationships, the feeling of being rejected, not being able to get ahead at jobs, and everything else that I had gone through, to lead me astray. These things were used by him to hold me back.

Once I understood the enemy's tactics, and what things were leading me astray, I started to change. This change led me to switch the music I was listening to. I started to stay out of the club also. And I kept asking God to change me slowly. I asked him to take away the things that were not of Him, and the very desire for those things.

In the past, I had gone to the altar plenty of times, but I never truly believed the true meaning of giving Him all of you. I didn't understand that it included giving him every pain that lies inside of me. I was only scratching the surface with what I was actually willing to trust Him with during those times. I now know that I should have trusted him with my life from the beginning because He laid down His life for me.

Now, even though I was still dealing with some things—still sad, still hurt, lost, and confused—I decided to continue to press forward. I started to believe the things that had been spoken over my life.

As I continued believing God for my healing, I moved back in with my aunt. My uncle had passed away, and she didn't want to live alone. So when she asked me to move back in, I happily said yes. It meant that I would have more space for me and my children. It also meant that I had someone to take me to my doctor's appointments.

During this time, I started to listen to Sarah Jakes Roberts every morning. It motivated me to listen to her story of where she had been and where she ended up. It helped me to keep going as I continued on my journey.

By this time, I could barely move my fingers. I had no range of motion in my wrist. But I continued to go to physical therapy. I kept reminding myself that I was not my situation. I was not just a girl who was disabled. I was going to overcome it. I was not going to live in pain for the rest of my life.

To help to alleviate my pain, the pain management doctor wanted me to try a ganglionic block. This meant that they would have to gain access to my neck to reach the nerve, I didn't want to have any procedure done. But I kept hearing, "trust the process." My church began to pray for my arm, and whatever procedure was coming up.

Ultimately, I decided to go along with the procedure. Even though I still thought in the back of my mind that nothing was going to work. Before they put a large needle in my neck, they gave me some valium. As the doctor watched on a screen, medicine was injected right into the nerve of my neck. Afterwards, the doctor told me that my limb could start working, and the pain should have been taken away.

As promising as the doctor's word had been, I had adverse effects to the medicine. I started to throw up. I felt weak. My voice even changed for a while. As a result of the failed procedure, the doctor decided that they were not going to do it again.

My doctor decided that the best, and last thing to do, was a spinal cord stimulator (this is a type of implant device that is used to send electrical signals to select areas of the spinal cord for treatment of certain pain conditions). Essentially, they placed a battery pack into my back that constantly sent electrical impulses to my nerves. The purpose of it was to help take away my pain. I was upset that I had to go through another procedure. I told God that I didn't want to have another surgery. I didn't want anything to go inside of my spine. I started to panic again. I freaked out. As I waited for the approval for the surgery, I kept hearing, "trust the process."

I was awake for the procedure. I lay flat on the table with my face down. They went into the cavity in my back with an epidural. I could feel them pushing something up inside of me. I could hear tissue ripping and popping. I could also feel it. It was very uncomfortable.

After about 30 minutes, to an hour, it was inserted. Afterwards, they had to keep doing x-rays to make sure that it was in the correct place. Followed by them programming and strapping the device to my stomach. They then taught me how to program the device.

Once I was home, my neck started to swell. I lay in bed the entire 7-day trial period. I couldn't even shower because of the open wires in my back, so I had to use baby wipes for cleaning. Thankfully, my aunt helped me during this time period. I had migraines. I was getting shocked so much that I had to call the company to reprogram it with a lower setting.

I endured the pain that started after the device was implanted because I wanted it to work. I wanted all the pain to be gone. I wanted to use my hands. I endured the pain I experienced while being propped up in the bed for five days. My own daughter had to help me by bringing me food to eat because I could barely walk.

When I went back to the doctor, I told him that I wanted the procedure to work, even though the back of my neck was extremely swollen. Yes, I had severe migraines, but I didn't really have much pain in my hand. They asked me to leave it in for a couple of more days because I was having better results. They pumped me full of muscle relaxers, hoping that the swelling in my neck would go down, and that I would be able to move more again. After I returned home from the doctor's, I mainly slept and took pain pills when I would wake up.

Returning to the doctor a couple of days later, I was asked to continue on for a couple of more days. I told the doctor yes because I was willing to try anything. After 8 days of more pain, we decided that it was best to remove the device.

Nothing appeared to be working. After eight months of physical therapy, there was no progress. My physical therapist had to let me go. It was bittersweet for me because going to the doctor's weekly had become such a big part of my life that I didn't know what I was going to do. Going to the doctor's had been a part of my routine. I felt like once I stopped going to the doctor's that I had lost part of my identity. I now felt like someone who had gotten hurt and thrown to the side.

With the physical therapy sessions no longer going, I was still doing a lot with a psychologist. I had to learn how to be a new person because of the injury. He explained to me about the process of where my mind was as I was going through everything and what to expect. He even said that it was great that I had my church family and the Lord to lean on during this process.

As doctors started to back away, I started to receive payment from workman's comp. I was grateful. But I still struggled with my pain.

I asked my pain management specialist to cut my arm off. I was serious. I couldn't use it anymore and it was causing me so much pain. He told me he couldn't because, with my disease, I would for sure have phantom limb syndrome. He encouraged me by saying that at any point, my arm could reactivate and come back just by bumping it, or falling on it. As he spoke, I thought in my head that I would be that person that it happened to because I was already told that I would be healed.

As I waited on my healing from God, I continued to smoke weed often to help me deal with the pain. I thought that smoking was better than taking those stupid pills or seeing people sexually. I was literally trying to fix some parts of my life, but not everything. I wanted to hold on to certain people as I went to church. I thought that because I was there, it was good enough because it was a big step for me.

I was going to church two to three times a week. While there, I would feel so convicted about the things that I was still engaging in. One day, as I spoke with one of my mentors, he asked me why I was smoking, and why I was posting pictures of me wearing revealing clothes. He asked, "are you walking in this life, or are you not? What are you watching?" I was shocked. Everything that he asked, and said to me, was the truth. I had been in church, but I wasn't fully committed. He told me that I had to let that stuff go and fully walk in all that God had for me.

I am so thankful that God placed my mentor in my life. No matter how much I called him crying about things, I was never judged, only encouraged. He always kept it real. This was something that I needed to remain focused on God.

Refocused, I began to go to church more. I started praying from a different place. I no longer prayed for what I wanted, but the things I heard from God. I had become a prayer warrior. I felt so honored that God had chosen me to intercede for others. With the urging of my pastor, I went from praying for 10 minute to praying for 30-40 minutes. The more I prayed, the more I heard clearly from God. I knew that I was stepping into something different.

I started to desire the Lord more. I wanted to hear the word more, so I would go to services and conferences offered by our sister churches. I wanted to be in God's presence as much as I could. As I continued to press forward and attend things, people kept speaking over my life. Their words were so positive and so beautiful. I was told I was breaking out, and that God was going to use me. People told me that the cards were stacked against me my whole life. I shouldn't have survived, and I did because God had a greater plan for me.

I was shocked that God would use me. Somebody who's done all this mess in my life. Somebody who had said they hated Him before. Knowing that God still wanted me, touched my heart.

I don't even know how to begin to describe how much I wanted the Lord in my life after those encounters. I continually asked him to break the generational curses over my life. I asked him to bring back my children. I told Him that I wanted to serve Him. I didn't drink anymore. I didn't go to the club. I stopped talking to men that I had no business entertaining. I literally began to separate myself from the things that I used to do. I separated myself from friends as well.

I became diligent with fasting and prayer. I started listening to different sermons all the time. I wanted a deeper relationship with God, so I stopped trying to have my feet in the world and in church. I fully gave Him everything. No, it wasn't easy, it was hard. I didn't want to throw away certain clothing, but I knew that I wasn't dressing like I should, so I got rid of them. I didn't want to have to give up certain friends and certain activities, but certain things didn't sit well with my spirit anymore.

As I went through the process of the scales falling off of my eyes, I went to the altar and cried. I left every tear and every heartache there. I'm sure people thought that I was crazy because I was constantly up at the altar, but I didn't care. I wasn't up there for anybody else. To me, it was just me and the Lord at that altar. I would tell him that I couldn't do it by myself. I asked him to show me the way as I threw my hands up in the air, as the tears flowed down my face. I kept going to the altar until I felt better and better.

CHAPTER 27: **SEX ADDICTION**

Being with Mr. Officer for all those years led to me getting used to being loved in the dark. It took me years to recover from him. During that time period, I was in and out of several relationships that went downhill. I had gotten involved with a married, but separated, man, and an engaged man. I had such low self-esteem that I kept allowing myself to be somebody's side chick. They didn't even know that I was using them and their homes to escape the pain that I felt, even if it was just for a moment in time. I didn't have to worry about not being able to pay bills, I placed all of that on the back burner. I used them as an outlet.

The honest truth is that I was using sex as an outlet. I know that you're probably thinking that I'm gross. It's okay if you do because I felt nasty. I believe that it all stemmed from my childhood abuse. I was so used to getting touched almost every night from such a young age, it almost became a part of me.

It caused me to masturbate at a young age. Whenever I needed to release, I became frustrated when I couldn't have an orgasm, or several orgasms. When I got older, I couldn't go through the day without watching pornography. I would literally lay in bed and watch it for hours like it was a normal tv show.

Even though I enjoyed watching it, I felt disgusted. I didn't even know why I would watch it all day long. I could have used that time to clean up or cook dinner. I was disappointed with myself, but I couldn't stop.

When I wasn't watching pornography, I was having sex. I felt that if I made the decision to have it myself, then there was nothing wrong with it. I felt that if I was making the choice to give my body to other people, even if it was for hours out of the day, they weren't using me. At the time, I honestly didn't know that I was a sex addict. I thought that it was normal to have sex multiple times a day for hours. I thought that was what men wanted. I felt that it's what made them like me more. That if I did the things that were in the videos that I watched, they wouldn't leave me.

Whenever I was with someone with a low sex drive, I would break up with them, or cheat on them. I had become so addicted to sex that I engaged in sex on the job. I had to do whatever I could to get that high I felt from the act of sex. It was less about the orgasm, and more about feeling the pain for me. I started to tell those I was involved with to not make love to me.

The trauma I experienced at a young age and its effects were already embedded in me. It did so much damage to me. I literally was put in overdrive sexually. I did not understand at the time that everything I was experiencing was what warfare was. But as I continue to walk with God, everything is making more sense.

I was held captive by the spirits of lust and perversion. That's why I spent so much of my time engaging in the sexual activities that I had been bound by. It wouldn't be until years later, when I learned about prayer and fasting from my pastor, that I was able to get a grip on the addiction that plagued me for many years.

1 Corinthians 6:19-20- "What? know ye not that your body is the temple of the Holy Ghost which is in you, which ye have of God, and ye are not your own"

After reading these scriptures, I started to understand that our bodies are not ours. I started to question myself about why I would sit there and defile my temple with all those images. I started to understand how they were disturbing my eye gates. I started to see that it was holding me captive. I even complained that I did not want to watch it, and still did.

I kept fasting and praying as I asked God to change me. I had to do it multiple times before I was freed. My freedom didn't happen overnight. It was gradual. I would start to feel convicted as I watched people sleeping with other people. I felt guilty if I masturbated. I lost the desire to have sex with random people. When this started to happen, I knew and could feel that God was working a change in me.

When I went to the altar during one service for prayer, I experienced a major shift. The man of God looked me in my face and told me I needed to give it up. He began to pray over me. I fell under the anointing of the Holy Spirit. As I lay there, something came over me. I decided to throw away all of the sex toys that I owned. And I stopped hanging around with certain men. I finally grew strong enough to cut them off, even though the enemy wanted me to stay bound and connected to them.

I was so thankful to God when he started to deliver me from being a sex addict. My addiction had taken me down the wrong path for years. I later learned that it was a roadblock that the enemy placed in front of me to keep me from getting to my assignment. While it was in my way, I couldn't get to where I needed to be.

Ephesians 6:12- "For we wrestle not against flesh and blood, but against principalities, against powers, against rulers of the darkness of this world, against spiritual wickedness in high places."

CHAPTER 28: MY MONSTER EX

Things that I had been previously told started to manifest. After four years of having lost my daughter to her father, she started living with me. I was happy my baby girl was home. It had not been done through the court and wasn't on paperwork, but she was with me. She made the decision to pack up her things and to move in with me because her father was still drinking a lot. I thank God that she moved back home with me because He knew that I needed her. I needed her more than she needed me. Thankfully, her father, although he usually did, didn't argue with me about it either.

Now that she was home, we were able to rebuild our bond. We began to do stuff together like we used to. I was relieved and grateful to have one of my children back home with me. The boys' father was still being evil and angry with me. Although they lived only two blocks away from me, he continued to tell me that I couldn't see them. But he had no issues calling me when he needed a babysitter.

Even though I knew that he only allowed me to see them when it was convenient to him, I would say yes. There were many times that I wanted to tell him that I wasn't my children's babysitter, I was their mother. But I held my peace.

When I had my children, I continued to be encouraging towards them. I let them know how much I loved them. I kept telling them that everything was going to turn around, but we had to have faith, and trust God and the process. I even took them to church with me as often as I could.

The truth is that it was hard at times for me only having one child at home. But I had to believe what I was told. I had to keep reminding myself that God was going to turn things around. So I kept thanking him in advance. I thanked him for protecting my children while they were away from me. I even anointed them before they left to go to their father's house.

I prayed without fully understanding how much of a monster the boys' father was. I didn't realize his evilness until my daughter asked me what my book was about. That night, she and I had just come back home from a conference. As we remained sitting in the car, I told her that one day she was going to read it. That answer wasn't good enough because she kept asking me questions. So I told her that it was about my life.

I told her that I had been through a lot of hurt and pain. I explained to her that losing them probably was the biggest pain. She then asked me if she was going to be in the book. I told her, "of course" because God told me to write the book and because they are a part of my life that I couldn't hold back. I then explained to her that there are a lot of things in the book that I don't want people to know about myself, but God required me to be raw, real, and open. That it was my testimony, and it was time for me to share the things that I had been through. I then told her that people will see how far God has taken me, and how He has turned my life all the way around.

When I was done speaking, I asked her "what's wrong?" I let her know that she could tell me anything. She looked at me with tears in her eyes and said, "I don't want to tell you; it's really bad." I held her hands as I told her that she could tell me everything, and that I knew that she had been keeping a secret. I then told her that if she was ready to talk, that I was ready to listen.

She began to cry as she revealed the horrific molestation (which I will spare you the details) that she endured at 7 years old. I pushed my seat all the way back in the car and she sat in my lap. That night we cried together. All I could think was, "why my child? Why this long and how? Why was this man living?"

I wanted vengeance. I wanted to kill him. It was way worse than I ever could have imagined. I couldn't believe that my child had endured months and months of being molested. I asked her if she was ready to go to the police. I truthfully told her that it wasn't going to be an easy process, but she had to tell her story. I encouraged her by telling her that, even though she feels like a victim, she's strong because she finally told me.

I couldn't even look at my child without imagining what she had to go through. It hurt to look at her. I felt like it had just happened yesterday, even though it had been seven years ago. I was in utter shock. I suspected something had happened to her years ago. But she wouldn't tell me or the police then. So nothing could be done. Now that I knew the truth, I blamed myself.

I had to do what was right. I decided that I was going to take her to DCFS, but it was closed, so I had to wait until Monday morning. The next morning, I tried to go to a barbecue and be "normal," but couldn't. I called my sister and the first thing she said was "let's go to church." That day, I went to the altar and cried. I felt sick and wanted vengeance. I had to fight against what I was feeling because the old me would have killed him. I had to fight the urge to drink. I wasn't going to go back.

I had to stay sane, but it was difficult. I was walking around in a daze in disbelief. I couldn't understand how somebody can do those things to a child. I couldn't understand why he treated me like I was the dirt on the bottom of his shoe, knowing what he has done to my daughter. I couldn't understand how he slept at night. Or, why my child!

It was hard for me not to be mad at God. It was hard for me to not throw everything that I had been through back at Him. I wanted to drink so bad, to drown my pain, but I knew that that was just the enemy wanting me to go back down the same path. Instead of giving in, I called on my pastor, and my mentor, for prayer. I even went back to the altar.

I had so much hate and anger in my heart. I didn't know how to give this to the Lord. I cried and asked him, "why Lord? why did it have to be this severe? Why did it have to be for that long? how did I not know?" My sister told me to rejoice in knowing that had I known what I now knew years ago, when I went to his house and ran that pole into him and kicked his door, I would be sitting in a jail cell. In that instant, I knew she was right.

I took my daughter down to the police station. We both gave our statements. Mine really didn't matter because I wasn't there for any of it. I merely repeated what I was told. When my daughter gave her statement, I watched how scared she was. He had threatened her. He told her that if she said anything that he would kill me.

I watched my child go through an emotional rollercoaster because she wasn't able to tell anybody what was going on. We didn't want to ruin the investigation. I wasn't even allowed to talk to her father about anything. This was hard because they had started to work together. I felt like he had a right to know. But I knew that he wasn't mentally stable. He would be furious and would end up sitting in a jail cell.

I did what was best for us all, I continued to act as if I didn't know anything, so that the boys' father would believe that he had gotten away with everything. When I had to see him get my boys for visitation, I tried to speak to him as little as possible. It was hard.

I kept asking God for strength and covering during the process. My daughter's case was considered an old case, therefore it wasn't a priority. I was told that it was going to take longer. I was angry.

My pastor started to explain to me that even this man who did this horrible thing to my child has a soul. I cried and I looked at my pastor and said, "I can't pray for him yet. I can't forgive him yet." Thankfully, my pastor understood. He never forced me.

It took a very long time to start praying for him. It was surprising to me that I could even pray for people who have done things like him. Honestly, I never thought that I would get to the point that I wouldn't hate him. I kept saying I was going to slap him one day, and saying that I hope that he got hurt in prison. But it was just my flesh talking.

The detective told us that things could take some time. He told us to be patient. Being patient was never something I was good at. I always wanted immediate results. But I knew I had to be patient because this was completely out of my hands. I tried my best to rely on God and to give the investigation to Him. But I couldn't help but to constantly call the police to check and see if he had gotten arrested.

I wasn't trusting the process. But I knew that I had to take my hand off of things and let God be God. I had to trust that it would all work out. So we all continued to pray.

CHAPTER 29: **DANNY**

That morning I woke up and decided that it was best that I got out of the house. I had been fighting the feelings of depression and anger. Everyone that I called to hang out with me couldn't. I didn't understand how everyone was too busy to go to the hot springs. It seemed like everything that I was trying to set up ended up getting canceled. I was highly annoyed.

In the midst of my failed plans, I received a text message that my son was taken to the hospital. I was puzzled when I responded, "what do you mean?" I was told that Danny kept having a lot of seizures back to back. My ex-husband said that he was getting in his car to go to the hospital. Immediately, I threw on some clothes and jumped in my car and drove 30 minutes to get to him.

I prayed and I cried as I drove. Suddenly, I got a call from his father again saying that he seemed to be doing better and that he was sleeping, so he wasn't going to take him in. I begged and pleaded with him to please just take him to the hospital. He hung up the phone after telling me that he was just going to keep in contact with me. I was angry. But I had no other choice but to turn my car around and drive back home.

A couple of hours later, my ex-husband called back. This time he said, "it's bad." I jumped back in my car again and drove towards the hospital. Once there, I sat waiting anxiously for them to arrive. As soon as he pulled up, he told me to get a wheelchair for my baby. I couldn't believe what I saw. My son was lifeless in a diaper.

He was slumped over in the back seat. I couldn't understand why my ex-husband had waited this long.

That day was the first time I had been really this close to him since finding out what he had done to my daughter. In that moment, I couldn't even think about being angry because my baby couldn't even hold his own head up. As my eyes moved across his body, I couldn't even grasp what I was looking at.

As soon as we entered the ER, they took us back. They took his vitals and called for the whole team. People started running in and out of the room sticking cords in my baby trying to get him to speak. Danny just laid there while they did multiple MRIs, x-rays of his chest, and asked a bunch of different questions.

We knew that he had had seizures. I was surprised to hear Josh say that he had had about 50. I was pissed when I heard that Danny had 50 seizures and he hadn't taken him to the hospital. I had to push my anger aside because it wasn't about what was done, it was now about my baby.

I kept crying to God, "God don't let my baby die. God I can't lose my child." After saying this, I asked God to have His way. I knew I had to rely on Proverbs 3:5, which states, "trust in the Lord with all thine heart and lean not unto thine own understanding." My son had still been unresponsive. I called my pastor crying. My pastor didn't hesitate to come to the hospital and pray for my baby with a lot of anointing oil on his hands. I couldn't help but to laugh.

The doctors were trying to find a bed in the NICU and the children's hospital that they were going to transfer him to. As my ex-husband argued with the hospital because he didn't want to pay for the ambulance ride for our son, my dad called to find out what was going on with my daughter's case. I broke down on the phone crying. At that moment, I couldn't worry about her case while Danny was being taken to the NICU. I instructed my parents to meet me at the hospital that Danny was being transferred to.

While I waited for Danny to be transferred, I had to keep walking in and out of the hospital room he was in. I couldn't sit there very long looking at my ex-husband's face. It angered me to be in the same room as the man who molested my daughter. I was torn because I wanted to be there for my son Danny.

When we were transferred to the children's hospital NICU, Danny's father left. I stayed because I wasn't working, and refused to leave my son until he had gotten out of the hospital. My son started to have violent seizures back to back. The doctors gave him so many different medications that it had to have been enough to knock out an obese man, but he continued to seize. Nothing was working. Every 3 to 4 minutes his body shook as he made groaning noises.

During this time, my parents arrived at the hospital. My father sat by Danny's side, my mother sat at the end of the bed, and I sat on the bed with my son. All night long, he continued to have seizures. They did brain scans throughout the entire night. They even talked about putting him in a medically induced coma. And considered flying him to a hospital in California.

Every time he had a seizure, my father sat talking to Danny. I did the same all night long, as I drank coffee to keep me up. As things got worse, I cried at his feet. The seizures lasted through the night until 6 in the morning.

As the doctors watched his scans, they realized that although he had many seizures, they had all been individual seizures. This turned out to be a good thing because his brain was getting a couple of minutes between the seizures to try to recoup.

He was still unresponsive when my family had to leave. I was grateful that I didn't have to deal with things alone. I had been very comfortable with them being there, although we didn't say much besides talking about Danny.

Even though I was going through this with my son, I decided that I couldn't just sit there and do nothing. When my sister came to the hospital, we anointed ourselves, the room, and our feet, and I began to walk the hallways. As I walked, I prayed for every child that was in the NICU. I put my own emotions aside as I leaned on my faith, and as we started to pray for my son.

Matthews 17:21- "Howbeit this kind goeth not out but by prayer and fasting."

My son had 100 seizures in less than a 24-hour period. I decided to go to church. I went to church in the same clothing that I had on when I went to the hospital. I looked torn up, but didn't care. When the people who followed me on Facebook, and knew what was going on with my son, saw me, they took me up to the altar. I stood there as a proxy for my son. They began to lay hands on me, speaking prayers over my child.

Later that day, my Bishop came to the hospital and prayed for my son. Another highly anointed man came on a different day to pray for him. Another Bishop that was in town during a revival, came to the hospital to pray for my son. A prophet also came to pray for him.

Aside from prayer, others came and showed acts of kindness. Some brought food. Others brought me socks and slippers. The outpouring of generosity and love was amazing. It was as if Danny was everyone's child laying in that hospital bed.

One day, as my sister prayed for my son, she went into deep intercessory prayer. She told my son to arise in Hebrew. My son sat up. We looked at each other and kept praying. Suddenly, Danny uttered the word "pray," and laid back down and went to sleep. I knew that it was nothing but God. Our prayers were being answered.

Once the doctors came back into the room, they explained that Danny had had one of the longest workouts of his life. They said he just needed to sleep. They were going to let him sleep as long as he could. It didn't matter if it was days. During the time that he slept, they continued to give him IVs and pump him with meds.

While his father came for a couple of hours during the daytime, I was able to go to the Ronald McDonald house to go shower and eat some food. I was able to return to church looking decent. There was a guest prophet that pointed me out and started to speak prophetically over my life. He told me that what looked like the end was just the beginning of my baby's life. I cried and jumped for joy after hearing this.

When I went back to the hospital that night, my son's eyes were open. He couldn't talk or walk at all. But he was now awake. From that point on, every day we saw more and more improvement. He started to speak a little bit. He became frustrated because he didn't have the same motor skills that he had before the seizures. He struggled to get his thoughts together also.

He finally started to try to walk. Danny now had a physical therapist, and a cognitive therapist, working with him. I saw my son go from lifeless to playing with balls, coloring, and trying to sing "All the Glory and All the Praise" church song. I joined in and would sing it to him, and he'd sing it back to me. I had a crazy praise during this time because of what all God had done.

I had so much to be thankful for. My son was a miracle. Every day he got better. He eventually started running down the hallway of the hospital. His speech started to improve, and he started to beg for food.

While I stayed for 10 days in Reno, my daughter stayed at home with my aunt. During this time, I felt like I was being a bad parent. I couldn't be at two places at one time. But children under a certain age were not allowed in the NICU. I also didn't want her there around the person who molested her either. I had no choice but to communicate with her through text and calls. I let her know that I loved her. I also gave her updates about her brother.

Once Danny was being moved from the NICU into a regular room in the hospital, I was relieved. It had been hard for me to sit in the same room with my ex-husband as he smirked at me. It had been nothing but God who gave me the strength to get through it. I know that I could not have done it on my own. I was learning self-control and patience. I had to be compassionate towards him because it was our child that was in the hospital.

Two days before my son got out of the hospital, my aunt called to tell me that I had to move out. I didn't even argue with her. I told her, "I'll talk to you when I get home." When I hung up, I began to cry again. I didn't know where I was going to go. I couldn't go live in an apartment with workman's comp checks. I had no idea when they were going to cut me off.

I began to seek the Lord again. It was almost Christmas time. My son was getting out of the hospital soon. I was still dealing with the situation with my daughter and my arm. God answered and said, "I told you to go home." I did not want to go home. I haven't lived there in a year. Yes, I was grateful for them moving me out of my house, and coming up to the hospital and sitting with me, but I never got along with them. I didn't want to be frustrated.

Every time I began to pray, God said, "go home." I called my sister to complain about what the Lord told me. I had a problem with being obedient. I couldn't understand why I had to go home. I didn't agree with things that came out of their mouths because it was rude and showed that they were close-minded. I was so confused on why I had to go home, but, honestly, I didn't see another option, even though my brother said I could move back in with him. I kept hearing go home.

I texted my dad because I couldn't even be grown up enough to pick up the phone and to call him. I was too nervous. It took a couple days, but they cleared out the big room for me. They put in bunk beds so that there would be plenty of space in this room for me and my children.

The time to pack up my stuff and move had finally come. My son was going home too. I couldn't be more happy. I was finally able to go home and see my daughter. I had missed her. When I saw her, I noticed that she was looking thinner. I hugged her and it hurt her. I didn't understand why. One day after school, she had a panic attack and threw up all over the bathroom. I asked her how long this had been going on. She told me since her brother was in the hospital.

My daughter was going through so much emotionally. Her brother being in the hospital, and me not being there to help her through what she was going through, led to her having anxiety attacks. I had no idea that she cried a lot while I was gone. Finding this out broke my heart. I started feeding her little by little. I let her know that she mattered, and that she was stronger than what she was going through. I told her that nothing was her fault. I also reminded her that I loved her and was on her side. I also enrolled us into counseling.

Once things became a little settled, and my son was feeling better, we went to church. That Sunday it was kid's Sunday. Danny got up and shared his testimony. As he spoke, his speech was still delayed. He became frustrated because he couldn't get the words out properly. But he finally said, "God told me in my ear I was going to live." The whole church started to praise and worship God. Tears started running down my face as he said there's nothing God won't do.

CHAPTER 30: TURN AROUND

When I moved back into my parents' house, I realized that God was softening my heart and teaching me how to truly forgive. It wasn't easy. I felt a little bit uncomfortable. It was awkward at first having two different religions. I had to go to my car and pray sometimes. But now I choose to no longer dim my light around them. They watch me go to my car and read my Bible. They see me taking my family to church. I don't explain to them that I am different. I don't even continue to hash out old problems. I allow them to watch and see for themselves.

I'm thankful to be home because I get to learn about my family through a different lens. I no longer see them through the lens of pain and a walled-off heart. I no longer see them through the lens of a child filled with anger. I can now see them for who they are, and for all of the positive things they have done for me. I see my father as being hilarious. I understand that my mother couldn't love me the way that I needed and wanted because she truly didn't know how to give or receive love.

Instead of continuing the cycle, I have decided to break it while I am there. I pray over her sick body often. I enjoy spending time with my family laughing and creating memories. I love sitting at the table with them playing board games and eating homemade cookies and fresh baked bread. It brings me so much joy and peace.

I now understand and am thankful that God sent me back home to heal and soften my heart. I love them differently now. I no longer just say "I love these people." I now say that I love them and love being at home with the family that God assigned to me.

I came to realize that God knew that I would be a foster child. He knew that I would get picked from a book at the orphanage and placed there. It's nice to have family time again. It feels good to laugh about the good times that I had in my childhood. It has also been nice being there while COVID-19 swept through the nation.

I thank the Lord for sending me back home. I really thought He was crazy at first. But after being home, I wish that I would have gone back without complaining. I wish that I would have humbled myself from the beginning. But I show myself grace and mercy because I know that I am a work in progress.

Even though things have not come full circle for me the way that I had wished by the ending of this book, I still celebrate where I am now. My divorce from my wife was finalized. I do not want to be in a lesbian relationship anymore. I've come to realize that I had engaged in that lifestyle because of all the bad experiences I had with men.

My son recently went to the doctor, and he is no longer having electrical discharges in his brain. There is no sign of seizure activity. Just like that, they are gone. I attribute this to prayer working! My son is now a happy child again. I know that it is nothing but God that did it. Because of this, I praise God like I never have in my life. It brings me so much joy to praise Him. He's so awesome. He really does deserve all of the glory!

Like my son, I have had so much great progress within my body. I rarely have any pain in my arm now. If I do too much, it gets a little bit sore, but nothing like before. I now take Tylenol occasionally for pain instead of pain pills. I've been dealing with CRPS for 15 months. In that time, I've come to the realization that what I thought was 15 months of pure hell really wasn't. Yes, I completely lost everything. But that's when I finally turned to the Lord.

That's when I finally put my hands up and I surrendered. I told the Lord that I could no longer live this life the way that I was living, and that I needed Him to guide me. I needed him to help me and to teach me. My ways weren't working anyways. I decided to fully obey God.

In doing so, I was no longer going to be angry. I wasn't going to let people's opinion of me hold me back. I wasn't going to let others tell me what I couldn't do when I am a child of God. With this, I realized that I was fearfully and wonderfully made.

Before, I didn't understand self-worth, or who I was. I only knew the trauma I was trying to survive. This was until I came to God. It was only after coming to God that I found my true purpose. It was only after that that I realized that my purpose, and the plan for my life, was already mapped out before I even got here. I finally realized that God had greater things for me, as long as I stayed on track.

Everything started to make sense. And with the power of prayer, layer by layer of healing started to take place in my life. All of those things that once haunted me, those things that even gave me suicidal thoughts, have finally fallen off.

I have changed so much about myself by the grace of God. But I'm still learning and growing in the Lord. Even as I release this book, I call myself a baby in Christ. Church has helped me to see the truth behind all the attacks that have occurred in life. Once I started to pray for deliverance, I asked God to soften my heart. I now understand that I was strong enough to go through everything because God had a purpose for me the entire time.

Even though I've made changes, there have been times during this process of growing in God that I've felt weak. In those times, I wanted to give up and throw in the towel. But God threw the towel back at me and told me to become stronger. He told me to hold on, even though I didn't understand why I went through these things. Looking back, I can honestly say that His grace got me through.

I never thought surviving trauma would become a part of my ministry. I never knew I even had a ministry inside of me. But even though I did not know, God knew. He knew that what I survived would cause me to want to help women; women who feel like they have nobody to confide in; women who are ashamed and embarrassed of the things they have done, or the things that have happened to them.

I recall laughing at myself in my drunk days and saying, "what haven't I been through. What girl has me beat." At that time, I used to be very insensitive to other people's stories. I pretty much laughed at them when they shared, as I said, "that's all you went through?" But now I want to help other women instead of putting them down.

Looking back now, I understand it's not about who's been hurt worse. We have all been through, and will go through, different things. It's about supporting each other, healing, forgiving, and letting go of guilt. It's about standing strong and becoming sisters in Christ. It's about understanding that we all are fearfully and wonderfully made in God's eyes, and marvelous are His works (Psalm 139:14).

EPILOGUE

The Lord knew the entire time that I was strong enough to go through what I've endured because I would have Him, as well as others who were willing to help get me through. He sent my sister in Christ, Laquitta, to keep pushing me to come to church. He sent my mentor, Dr. Jonathan Mason, who never judged me, but allowed me to cry and get things out before telling me the raw truth. He sent my spiritual family, Toni and Laquitta, who are my home away from home.

He sent my pastor, and First Lady, Brown, to parent me. They showed me affection and hugged me when needed. They encouraged me when I was feeling discouraged. I can honestly say that if it weren't for them, I wouldn't be as far as I am in my relationship with God. Or as strong as I am, as I continue to on my journey.

The court situation with my daughter is still being investigated. It feels like it's taking longer than it should. Oftentimes, when I get frustrated, I just pray to the Lord. I had to start trusting Him with this situation completely. I even started to pray for my ex. I asked the Lord to help me forgive him, and to have mercy on his soul. I even asked that He would turn his life around. I never once thought I would pray for the man who hurt my daughter. The one who ruined my family. But I understood what my pastor said that he has a soul too.

I have faith that God is working out that situation. I just keep saying, "no, it's not my battle, it's the Lord's." So I continue to keep my hands off of the whole situation, as I continue to seek counsel and prayer.

As I continue to give things to God, things that were prophesied to me years ago are unfolding right before my eyes. I now have more than enough money, because of my injury, to pay for a lawyer to get my children back. It had been prophesied to me years ago that I was going to get a check. Now that I had it, I was going to start the process of getting my children back. But the Lord told me no. Suddenly, I felt the need to stand still. I didn't argue about it this time.

I had grown enough to know that the Lord was still trying to fix some things on my behalf. He started taking me to a higher place with Him around this time. I started to gain more knowledge of His word. I began to read my Bible even more. He had me stretch outside of my comfort zone when I started a prayer line.

I've become a completely different person. Now people turn to me for advice. I am stronger than I have ever been in my life. I'm no longer battling depression and anxiety. I'm no longer an alcoholic. When I'm frustrated, I just speak to my Father, and I wait for Him to tell me what to do. Now I walk by faith. I ask the Lord before I do anything, and I thank Him for His mercy.

I never thought I would be that church girl singing, dancing, and waving a flag for His glory. I thought that was for the old ladies with the big hats, and the people who've never really been through anything in life. Boy, was I wrong! I actually want to be involved in church, and live my life surrendered to God more than ever.

During this process, men started coming out of the woodwork randomly. I am proud to say that I didn't respond like the old me. I turned down their invitations instead of giving in just to get a couple of free meals and somebody to talk. Even when I started to get involved with a man in church, I turned away because I realized it wasn't my time. I stood firm on my desire to wait on my God sent husband (whom I diligently pray for) in every way, including with my body.

I placed my need to continue my walk with God over my own desires. Besides, God gave me a specific time when I would meet someone. I've decided until that time came, I wasn't going to entertain random men, or allow different distractions to creep in.

1 Corinthians 10:13 (ESV) -"No temptation has overtaken you that is not common to man. God is faithful and he will not let you be tempted beyond your ability, but with the temptation he will also provide the way of escape, that you may be able to endure it."

For the first time in my life, I am single. But I've grown to realize that I am not alone. The truth of the matter is that I was never alone and will never be alone. I just had to learn how to trust in God and lean on Him. I've learned the importance of calling on Him in the time of need, instead of my best friend, or a man. And you know what? God never ceases to amaze me.

As I look back at my entire life, I continue to think about what if I would have come to Him sooner. I was stubborn back then, thinking that I knew what I was doing with my life. When in actuality, I didn't.

Even though I wonder about this, I'm okay with where I am. I now know that even though I battled back then, I am no longer held captive, and will not be held captive ever again. I've come to understand that if you seek God enough, and ask Him for help with a sincere heart, there's nothing that He won't do for you.

2 Corinthians 5:17- "Therefore, if any man be in Christ, he is a new creature: old things are passed away; behold, all things are become new."

Knowing that my slate has been wiped clean, and my old mess is gone, has changed me. Realizing that I have been forgiven, when I was on a fast track to hell as I took people with me, is a blessing. It makes me want to bring people up with me. I want others to experience this life that I am now living. I want all to know that there is a light on the other side of pain and trauma. That God can turn your heart around, and you too can experience real joy and peace.

I'm excited for what the future holds for me. Everything is being turned around in God's timing. I'm excited for where He is taking me. I'm sober. I'm celibate. I'm happy that I have the Holy Ghost. I'm happy that I am an overcomer. I'm happy that there is purpose in my pain, and that I've Survived Trauma . . .

ACKNOWLEDGMENT

First, I have to give honor to God. I just thank Him for being the head of my life and bringing me through all my adversities

I thank my 3 amazing children. Each and every one of them has a special place in my heart. I encourage you all to follow Christ, and your dreams will come true!

I definitely couldn't have come this far without my mentor, Dr. Jonathan D. Mason, a true Kingdom builder. He was one of the first people who did not give up on me 8 years ago. Because of him, his loving kindness, and open-door policy, my life has forever been changed.

I thank my spiritual parents, Pastor Gregory Brown, and First Lady Brown, for being such genuine humble servants. They loved and taught me so much. As I was transforming, they didn't see my sin. Instead, they saw me as a woman of God. I couldn't ask for anybody better; they have truly been a blessing to me and my children's lives. I love them.

I also give thanks to my Greater New Refugee church family, Elder Drew, Sister Laquitta, Sister Toni, Sister Casey, Pastor Bob, and Sister Valerie. Thank you for the love and support, and always being *for* me, and not *against* me. I'm grateful that God strategically placed every single one of you in my life, whether it was for prayer, teaching, or just leading by example. You all have a special place in my heart! Sister Toni, thanks for opening up your home as a safe haven for me. And Sister Casey, thanks for being the fountain that just kept pouring.

Laquitta and Shurrie, thank you for being a big part of my journey. Thank you for loving me and allowing me to be the woman of God that I am trying to be. Thank you for tying my shoes when I wasn't able to; driving me to doctor's appointments, and just being a shoulder to cry on. You ladies are amazing. And I love you and your children forever.

My brothers, Roy, Marcel, and Chance, even though life tried to separate us, I'm thankful that God brought us together. I love you all. Don't ever give up on yourself, and always remember that you all have a purpose.

My adopted family, thank you for the ride. I love you all from the bottom of my heart. And I'm enjoying our new adventures together.

CONTACT TACHIANNA

FACEBOOK: Tachianna Ortis

EMAIL: Tachianna27@gmail.com

Made in the USA
Middletown, DE
27 September 2020

20433794R00129